My Russia

Photographs supplied by the author follow p. 6.

My Russia

The Political Autobiography of
Gennady Zyuganov

Edited by
Vadim Medish

M.E. Sharpe
Armonk, New York
London, England

Library of Congress Cataloging-in-Publication Data

Ziuganov, G. A. (Gennadii Andreevich)
My Russia : the political autobiography of Gennady Zyuganov / by
Gennady A. Zyuganov : edited by Vadim Medish.
p. cm.
Articles and excerpts from earlier books; also includes the full
text of his book, "Russia and the contemporary world"—Editor's note.
Includes index.
ISBN 1-56324-995-2 (alk. paper)
1. Ziuganov, G. A. (Gennadii Andreevich) 2. Presidential
candidates—Russia (Federation)—Biography. 3. Politicians—Russia
(Federation)—Biography. 4. Russia (Federation)—Politics and
government—1991– I. Ziuganov, G. A. (Gennadii Andreevich).
Rossiia i sovremennyi mir. II. Title.
DK510.766.Z58A3 1997
947.086′092—dc21   96-39545
[B]   CIP

Printed in the United States of America

The paper used in this publication meets the minimum requirements of
American National Standard for Information Sciences—
Permanence of Paper for Printed Library Materials,
ANSI Z 39.48-1984.

∞

BM (c) 10 9 8 7 6 5 4 3 2 1
BM (p) 10 9 8 7 6 5 4 3 2 1

Contents

Editor's Note

It has been said that proponents of capitalism tend to underestimate the good in human nature while believers in socialism, on the other hand, overestimate the same human quality. Does it follow that the former will enjoy lives full of pleasant surprises while the latter become embittered by betrayals and disappointments?

Gennady Andreevich Zyuganov is a socialist, a communist, who, at age 52, has had his share of disappointments. But, by all evidence, he has not been embittered by this experience. Moreover, he has so far been spared disillusionment in another area of high risk—his idealization of the Russian people, Russian history, and just about everything else Russian.

Zyuganov's ability to combine socialist ideas with Russian nationalism —the so-called "red–white" formula—deserves our attention, although it is by no means unique or unprecedented. In fact, this formula, more by necessity than by choice, was at the base of the Soviet system, enabling it to last as long as it did. Zyuganov's new version of the old recipe tries to make virtue out of necessity and is, at least for the time being, more white and less red.

Zyuganov's political autobiography tells the story of how he arrived at this position. As recounted here, it consists of five main parts.

The first contains a brief autobiographical sketch and some essays on selected topics that sum up Zyuganov's credo. This selection includes an article that originally appeared in *The New York Times* and deals with American-Russian relations.

The second part contains articles and excerpts, selected by Zyuganov, from his book *The Drama of Power* (1993). It will help the reader to understand how he reacted to Mikhail Gorbachev's perestroika, the collapse of the Soviet Union, and Boris Yeltsin's initial reforms, and how his thinking on other subjects evolved during those years.

The third part presents in full Zyuganov's more recent book, *Russia and the Contemporary World*, published in Russia in 1995. This book is the expression of Zyuganov's thoughts and ideas during the years immediately prior to the presidential elections in Russia (June–July 1996), when he successfully built his coalition of "National Patriotic Forces." Formed around Zyuganov's Communist Party of the Russian Federation (CPRF), this movement includes more than 200 large and small political groups. Among the former are the Agrarian Party and groups led by Nikolai Ryzhkov, Alexander Rutskoi, Stanislav Govorukhin, and Viktor Anpilov, all of whom supported Zyuganov in the 1996 presidential elections.

Today Zyuganov is concurrently chairman of both the Communist Party and the "National Patriotic" opposition movement. He is also the leader of the large communist faction in Russia's parliament, the State Duma.

The fourth part consists of two important presidential election campaign documents written by Zyuganov—his economic program and his election platform. The two statements propose specific measures to pull Russia out of socioeconomic crisis.

The fifth part of the book covers Zyuganov's reaction to the outcome of the presidential election. It is not a postmortem. Zyuganov's "snowball" theory, based on the ever-growing numbers of ballots cast for him over the past three years, lends credibility to his optimistic predictions about his political prospects. Not surprisingly, Zyuganov does not think much of another theory of Russia's possible political future that—using the metaphor of a "drying-up well"—argues that projected demographic changes bode ill for the strength of the red–white voting bloc over the next few years.

Which of the two scenarios Russia is more likely to follow is difficult to predict at this time. It is an equation with many unknowns.

Prominent among them are the state of the economy and of Boris Yeltsin's health. We know that getting reelected took a great deal of effort on the part of the enfeebled Yeltsin. One might wonder whether any of Yeltsin's "democratic" heirs-apparent could match this performance. This book by Zyuganov offers readers an opportunity to assess another of the players in Russia's ongoing political drama, one who is still undeniably a potential successor to the top position in the Kremlin.

* * *

Is Gennady Zyuganov a communist, a socialist, or a social democrat? Should his own word on the subject serve as a definitive answer? And how much does such a self-designation really matter? After all, the system that existed in the Soviet Union was officially called "socialism" (not "communism"), and for the first twenty years of its existence, Lenin's party included the words "social-democratic" in its name. Zyuganov calls himself a communist, but he also insists that he stands for (1) religious freedom, (2) democratic political pluralism, and (3) regulated private property and business. A dozen years ago, a Soviet citizen professing just one of these beliefs would have been promptly expelled from the Communist Party and could have faced a much worse fate.

It is also an open question whether Zyuganov wants to move Russia forward or backward. This book does shed some light on the subject, but it is not necessarily a true compass. If Russia is to be moved forward, Zyuganov insists that this must be done strictly on Russian terms. He does not equate modernization with Westernization, just as he rejects the notion that there was nothing positive in Russia's past, both before and during the Soviet era. If Russia is to be moved backward, how far back would this movement go? Zyuganov writes approvingly of several phases of Soviet history, including the period of Lenin's New Economic Policy in the 1920s and the early years of Gorbachev's perestroika. His role model as a leader is Lenin.

Zyuganov, of course, considers the demise of the Soviet Union a major tragedy. He offers three theories of why it happened. The "natural-death" scenario refers to the accumulated failures of an obsolete empire over several years. The "assisted-suicide" scenario puts the blame on the inept and vain leaders of the perestroika era. And the "assassination-plot" scenario darkly hints at overseas conspirators helped by inside "agents of influence." Zyuganov's innate realism supports the first two scenarios, but his flare for political dramatics nudges him toward the last one.

In international relations, Zyuganov rejects America's claims to global hegemony and its efforts to promote a "new world order." He wants Russia—or rather, a voluntarily reconstituted version of the Soviet Union—to act as the geopolitical center in Eurasia, one of the components of a multipolar world. In a sense, he wants to restore "a Russia that can say no."

* * *

Almost the entire text of Zyuganov's self-described political autobiography, including his two books, is a compendium of articles, interviews, and speeches. At times this imparts to the text a journalistic flavor of quick reaction to unfolding events or snatches from a dialogue. At the author's request, special care has been taken to preserve in translation the author's own style of expression and, more important, his way of thinking and reasoning. To the extent that this is deemed necessary, endnotes and brief editor's comments are provided to clarify the historical background. The former are located at the end of each part, and the latter are enclosed in brackets in the text. A glossary of Russian terms and a brief chronology of events are also provided at the end of the book.

Vadim Medish
Professor Emeritus
American University
Washington, DC

A Letter from the Author

Dear American Readers:

Russia and America must know each other better. This, I believe, will guarantee that the cold-war era can never return. We are two great countries, two great peoples. We have our own historical destinies, our own cultures, our own national values. We both have much to be proud of. So let us strengthen our dialogue through various channels—culture, science, economics, and politics—not suppressing or opposing but rather complementing and enriching each other.

Our paths of development may differ. Historically, each of our countries has found its own solutions by taking into account the specific features of the national psychology of its people and the peculiarities of its self-awareness and culture. But that should not stand in the way of our coming closer together.

During centuries of their existence, the peoples of Russia have created their special world—the world of Russian civilization. Since the long-ago times of paganism, we have been cultivating our land, harvesting grain, planting gardens, building temples. The Russian fields have nourished our warriors, builders, artists, and cosmonauts. We have gathered our people into one nation, built our own statehood, and served as a shield protecting Europe from the devastating invasions of barbarians. We developed our communal principles of life because we could not have survived otherwise in the vast Eurasian expanse and the severe northern climate. Today, an Orthodox church and a spaceship are the symbols of the Russian dream.

You have gone your own way, relying on your own religions and your own national ideas and values.

But we also have important things in common: the vast size and the multiethnic complexion of our countries. Russian talents have left their deep marks in your country. Among them were television inventor Vladimir Zworykin and helicopter designer Igor Sikorski. There were likewise Americans who came to Russia to help us in our difficult times, including the remarkable American journalist John Reed, whose remains rest in the Kremlin wall. America admires Dostoevsky and Tolstoy, Stanislavsky and Chekhov, and my generation of Russian readers is in debt to Hemingway, Faulkner, Steinbeck, and Updike.

At the threshold of the third millennium, both of our countries look to the future. This is not the time for mutual charges directed against each other for past transgressions, whether the annihilation of the Indians and the slave trade or the destruction of the peasantry and the GULAG. We should be frank and fair with each other. It would be unjust to equate today's Americans with slave traders and slave owners solely because of their history. But it would be just as unforgivable to label contemporary Russian communists as former prison guards. The history of any nation cannot be purged of even its most tragic pages. We must learn from history and use its experience for our advancement toward a better future.

Both America and Russia have gone through unique historical experiences. Our countries both lived through destructive civil wars and yet managed to stay together as unified nations and, in time, to become the world's two great powers. This distinction puts a special responsibility on us to act wisely and with restraint.

There is nothing that really divides us—no disputed territories or religious or ethnic conflicts. In historical terms, both of our nations are young. Both are full of energy, strength, and vitality. Together, we have enormous scientific, technical, and cultural potential. We should not fight but cooperate and, at the same time, peacefully compete with each other. As history teaches us, such competition serves as a powerful stimulus for global development. It also assures humankind of having a continued choice of alternatives.

The world does not need an "iron curtain," but this does not mean that the whole world should be exactly the same. We believe that it was a serious mistake to try to impose the Soviet model of development on certain countries of Europe and Asia. Every country should be allowed to determine its own path of development, borrowing or rejecting the experience of others. In the past, our two countries borrowed and learned from each other, and they should continue to do so in the future.

But at the same time, let Russia be Russia and let America be America. Ours is a big and diverse world. We should not try to destroy and level this diversity; rather, we should ensure, through tolerance and compromise, that diverse and unique civilizations coexist peacefully with each other.

Today, Russia finds itself in a complex economic situation. Our country is going through a difficult phase of history. We communists oppose the ruling regime in Russia because we disagree with its course of socioeconomic reforms. The main reason for our disagreement is our belief that this course of reforms either underplays or completely ignores Russia's national specific features, depending instead on Western models. We support reforms, but we believe that to succeed they must be based on Russia's own historical experience and traditions.

There are many things in America that I like. They range from American patriotism to American efficiency. I appreciate your respect for your own unique history, your culture, and the importance of self-reliance. And I ask you to be just as open-minded in your opinions about my native country—Russia—by learning more about it. I would like to help you.

This book, which I offer to American readers, is a step in that direction. The book explains the current situation in Russia and our struggle to pull the country out of its crisis, revive its spirit, and heal its wounds. The book also talks about the new Communist Party of the Russian Federation and about how this party, as part of a broad popular opposition, is striving to expedite Russia's recovery.

Gennady Zyuganov
Moscow
August 18, 1996

My Russia

Part 1

A Russian Communist

Who I Am and What I Believe

This material was written and published between late 1993 and the presidential elections of June–July 1996. Included here are two major components: Zyuganov's autobiographical sketch (1996) and fifteen topical commentaries compiled from different published sources, including an op-ed article from The New York Times. *Together, these essays summarize Zyuganov's "red–white" credo, which combines socialist ideas and Russian nationalism. According to Zyuganov, Russians have always associated socialism with traditional concepts of community that are deeply rooted in their unique national mentality.*

—V.M.

About Myself

I am Russian by blood and spirit and love my Native Land.

I was born in 1944 in a place that has a special meaning for Russia. When a rooster crows in our village of Mymrino, he can be heard in three adjacent regions: our own Orel Region and the neighboring regions of Briansk and Kaluga. This juncture lies on the border of the steppe and the forest between the Oka and Volga Rivers, which is the birthplace of the Russian nation.

I come from a family that has produced three generations of teachers. Although some family members were and others were not communists, they all shared these two characteristics: working hard from morning until evening and, almost without exception, fighting for their country. Many did not return from the last big war. My father, Andrei, lost his leg in the battle for Sevastopol.

I had my first job while still in high school, and, after graduating with distinction, I worked for a year in my school as a teaching assistant. Then my village collective sent me to a teacher's college in Orel. I consider teaching to be a profession worthy of respect and esteem. In my family virtually everyone teaches, either in school or at the college level. Together, we could educate a young person under one roof, so to speak. Among us are mathematicians, physicists, literary scholars, and historians. By the way, my own first teacher was my mother, Marfa, who taught elementary school for forty years. I remember that in my four years as her pupil I only once called her "mother" in class; she was strict and demanding.

During my sophomore year in college, I was drafted into the army. I served in a radiation and biochemical reconnaissance unit (in East Germany), which was not something to be envied. Of my three years of military service, one year was spent wearing a gas mask and a protective rubber suit; I burned three pairs of boots saturated with radiation.

In 1966, while serving in the army, I joined the Communist Party of the Soviet Union (CPSU), believing that the communist idea, which is over two thousand years old, most profoundly expresses people's needs and hopes. It is in accord with the Russian traditions of communality and collectivism, which meet the fundamental interests of my country.

Upon being discharged from the military, I completed my studies in

3

physics and mathematics at Orel Teacher's College, went on to do graduate work at the Academy of Social Sciences in Moscow, and defended my dissertation in philosophy. This enabled me later to teach higher mathematics and philosophy at the college level.

I have been married to my wife, Nadezhda, for over thirty years. We have two grown-up children—a son, Andrei, and a daughter, Tatiana—both of whom are married and are pursuing their professional careers. We have two grandsons, Leonid and Mikhail. At this time, three generations of our family, including my widowed mother, our daughter, and her husband, share one apartment in Moscow.

As for my career in the Party apparatus, I tried my hand at virtually every single rung of the CPSU Central Committee on Old Square in Moscow. As part of my duties there, I traveled extensively over the entire country, from its western borders to Sakhalin Island and from the Baltic Sea to Central Asia. During my last ten years at the Central Committee, as one of the handful of party officials assigned to the special "War Contingency File," I personally investigated every social upheaval in the country, thus gaining first-hand experience in dealing with emerging major problems.

In my capacity as a deputy chief of the CPSU Ideological Department working on Russian problems, I actively supported the idea of creating a separate Russian Communist Party as a party that would protect Russia's national state interests within the CPSU. This idea was opposed by Mikhail Gorbachev and his crew, who at that time, rather than debate our arguments, mounted a vicious propaganda campaign trying to discredit me and other Russian communist leaders.[1]

I have much to repent. First of all, I blame myself for not finding the time and the opportunity to expose fully the mafia-like political structure of the CPSU, at the very top level of which I worked. I have much to repent because already in the late 1980s my colleagues and I working on Central Asia had evidence that a blood bath, which could have cost some 100,000 lives, was in the making in Tajikistan.[2] By the same token, my colleagues and I who were involved with the Caucasus warned the Georgian leadership and others that if their unchecked rush for sovereignty were to spill over the borders, they would face the same situation that had existed some two hundred years earlier, before the treaty that voluntarily joined the area with Russia.[3] I also worked on the issue of rising crime in the country, unsuccessfully trying to put it on the agenda of the Politburo. The top political leaders likewise preferred not to deal with problems in the Armed Forces and with the situation in the Baltics. All warning signals, like mine, were swept under the rug and ignored.

As a communist who joined the Party for ideological reasons, I wholeheartedly welcomed perestroika and did my best to expedite its advent. The Soviet model of socialism was in urgent need of a qualitative change. But during the past decade our country has been twice deceived and betrayed: first by Mikhail Gorbachev and his immediate cohorts, who, while promising needed reforms, destroyed the Soviet Union and all its structures; and then by Boris Yeltsin, who finished the job under the cover of idle talk about "democracy" and a "market economy."

It was against this tragic background that I became one of the leaders of the opposition. Early in 1996, I accepted the nomination to run for the presidency of Russia as the candidate of the National Patriotic coalition, which includes the Communist Party of the Russian Federation (CPRF). Unfortunately, I did not win, although approximately 30 million people—more than 40 percent of those who voted—cast their ballots for me.

At present, I serve concurrently as chairman of the Communist Party of the Russian Federation and of the National Patriotic Union "Russia," which is the new name of our united opposition movement. I am also the leader of the CPRF faction in the State Duma.

About Socialism

The entire history of humankind in the twentieth century demonstrates that we should move forward to socialism. And in doing so, we should not discard the positive experience of the past but rather thoroughly analyze it and adopt what was good in it.

The goal of a society of social fairness emerged long before Marxism, and the realization of that ideal has enlisted followers of different ideologies, from Christian socialists to anarchists. The socialism that was built in the USSR and a number of other countries was, of course, far from perfect. But it exhibited some historic achievements. The socialist system enabled us to create a powerful state with a developed national economy. We were the first to venture into the cosmos. Our culture reached unprecedented heights. We were justly proud of our

achievements in science, theater, film, education, music, ballet, literature, and the visual arts. Much was done to develop physical culture,
sports, and folk arts. Every citizen of the USSR had the right to work,
free education and medical care, and a secure childhood and old age.
Appropriate budgetary allocations subsidized housing and provided for
the needs of children. People were sure of their tomorrow. A workable
alternative to capitalism was created in our own country and in other
socialist countries. This was the concrete historical justification of the
socialist path of development.

Not even our ideological opponents can understand why we ourselves destroyed that which in many ways was working so well. Today
we are calling for a renovated socialism free of deformities and fatal
errors and mindful of everything modern and progressive that humankind has created.

Why Did Soviet Socialism Fail?

I believe that our people have never rejected socialism. They were
simply deceived by demagoguery and false promises. Remember
Gorbachev's and Yakovlev's vocabulary during the past ten years?[4]
They used to say "More democracy—more socialism," "For socialism
with a human, democratic face," "Perestroika is continuing what was
started by the Great October Revolution," "Reforms are taking
Russia's socialism to the level of modern civilization," and so forth.
Everything that was being done in the name of these and similar slogans was taken by the people at large to mean not the destruction but
the improvement of socialism. After all, these slogans were proclaimed
by persons commanding the respect of the Party and the nation. They
were the highest-ranking leaders in the country, whose honesty was
taken for granted.

A majority of the people, under the stress of events, mistook populist demagoguery for the expression of national consensus. By the
mid-1980s, there was much disappointment with the slow economic
development and the stiffening bureaucratization of the Party and the
state administration. Millions of citizens felt alienated from state affairs because the Party monopolized power and minimized the role of
the soviets [elected councils].

It is clear now that a decisive role in the destruction of the country

On active military duty in East Germany.

Zyuganov (left) with his graduating class.

In younger days.

A visit to Red Square. From left: uncle, father, son Andrei, mother, Zyuganov (man at right unidentified).

Dancing with daughter Tatiana.

At the summer house.

Zyuganov helping his daughter and his mother at the kitchen table.

A picnic.

With daughter Tatiana, wife Nadezhda, and cat (Basil).

The candidate.

was played by a subjective factor—the weakness and incompetence of the leaders then in power. Those people displayed personal cowardice, which later turned them into traitors and led to a degeneration of a part of the ruling elite.

It is widely agreed that the crisis, caused by a power struggle at the top, was cleverly used by foreign intelligence services and centers of ideological warfare.

Objective reasons contributed to the defeat of socialism. Socialism had failed to realize its full potential in such important areas as labor productivity, the well-being of average workers, and the involvement of broad masses of the people in the creative process. Russia had been drawn into an exhausting arms race, and, in trying to catch up economically with the West, we fell into imitating Western values and observing Western priorities.

On Reforms

The radical reforms started in January 1992[5] have brought catastrophic results. Today it is clear that the real goal of the "reformers" was the destruction of Russia's economy under the slogan "The state must be removed from managing the national economy." The country has been deeply damaged by the principle that calls for maximum exports of raw materials and semifinished goods and encourages unlimited imports of food and industrial products.

As a result of this grave distortion, gross domestic output has declined by 40 percent. The production base of the economy and the network of economic ties have both been undermined. Enterprises are forced to reduce the volume of production radically because of declining orders and purchases, shrinking investments, unrealistic prices, and their diminishing ability to compete.

The foundation of our agriculture has been virtually destroyed. Agricultural production has been decreased by one-third. Our country has lost its food security and become dependent on foreign imports: 54 percent of the food consumed in Russia (70 percent in its urban centers) comes from abroad.

Forced privatization was conducted without regard for laws and elementary fairness. As a consequence, the rights of the new owners have not been duly legalized. Nor have these rights been morally justified in the eyes of society. A lacerating social division has split our people into the super-rich and the very poor; the middle class, which used to ensure social stability, has disappeared.

Official documents show that 500 of Russia's largest industrial enterprises, realistically valued at no less than 200 billion U.S. dollars, were privatized and sold for about 7.2 billion U.S. dollars by the end of the first stage of privatization. These bargains ended up in the hands of foreign companies or their front structures [surrogates].

Reform is a natural condition of society. Every society carries out reforms continuously. At this time, in the process of reforming our politics, we should find a balance among the branches of power and make sure that the government as a whole serves the people. In the economic sphere, we must find the best, most appropriate proportions of state, collective-cooperative (share) ownership, and private forms of property.

Reforms must ensure an opportunity to create freely. Since truth is born out of disputes, reforms must secure freedom for political competition within the bounds of strict adherence to the law and to the exclusion of attempts to undermine the social, spiritual, and moral principles of our life. At the same time, the basic values, obligatory for all, must be clearly defined.

On Democracy

Today's so-called democracy [in Russia] amounts to the right of citizens and parties to say what they please and the government's right not to listen. But with real democracy, state bodies must be responsible to the people. The president and the government are not responsible because nothing controls them, and the parliament is neither responsible nor accountable—because it has no rights.

We must amend the Constitution and move toward a political system in which the president is not a "tsar" or "father of the nation" but the highest official in the service of society, under the control of and accountable to the people's elected representatives.

Today the president is not subject to any control and not accountable to anybody. The tsars were at least afraid of God, but Yeltsin is not afraid even of God. He plays the role of a judge, a prosecutor, and a benefactor. He appoints and fires anyone he pleases, and he is not held liable for anything.

The government is not controlled by the legislature. Real power is concentrated in the hands of those around Yeltsin. This is the "second government," which issues decrees, writes directives, engages in political manipulations, and arbitrarily disbands, forbids, or uses force.

No minister should be appointed without the approval of the legislative branch. The parliament and deputies must be held accountable to the electorate. All bodies, from the bottom to the top, must be regularly elected. Freedom plus justice constitutes humanism.

On a Free Market and Private Property

We advocate effective protection of the economy now in existence in Russia. We are for an economy in which there is a place for a powerful state sector, collective property, and private property, including that which *legally* belongs to foreign investors.

Private property is completely acceptable in farming, services, trade, small and medium-sized production, and some other business undertakings.

We should have a positive attitude toward entrepreneurship. But we should remember that only 5–7 percent of the population is inclined to engage in their own business. The majority want to continue to work as office clerks, doctors and nurses, teachers, and policemen, just as before. It would not do to push them all out into the street and force them to sell cigarettes.

The term "market economy" has been seriously compromised. We should instead be thinking about a mixed economy developed in ways that are most acceptable to our people and protected by just and reasonable laws.

We guarantee the inviolability of work-earned private property created by honest personal labor or the labor of one's family. We should use legal means against the growth of any kind of monopoly or of other ways of exploiting and subordinating citizens.

Church and Religion

Russian culture in general and the Orthodox Church in particular are currently the targets of constant attacks by the opponents of our statehood.

Even Stalin, having understood the deep roots of our statehood, rehabilitated the church and once even raised a toast to it. But the ideological hostility to religion persisted. It is no accident that Khrushchev, the precursor of perestroika, struck a heavy blow against both folk peasant culture and the Orthodox Church.

We deeply respect the faith of our ancestors. In the new Program and Rules [the founding documents of the Communist Party of the Russian Federation], we have deleted all antireligious notions and spelled out that religious convictions are the private business of every person.

Our current rulers superficially honor the church and show themselves on television standing in churches and holding candles. But take a look at their actual policy. So why did our current government not confirm the bill limiting the activities of foreign religious sects? Why did they receive leaders of the Aum Shinrikyo sect and the Moon [Universal] Church? Why do they patronize Scientology? Who has allowed all kinds of foreign preachers to use our television? The Orthodox Church is under an intense offensive by these foreign religions, which clearly enjoy the support of the current regime.

It is very important that the religious cultures of the Russian and other peoples of our country be able to reassert their legitimate rights. In this way, the historical truth and the historical memory of the people are restored. Regardless of whether they adhere to religious or materialist convictions, most people now recognize the positive role of churches, monasteries, nunneries, and religious leaders in the development of culture and in the dissemination of literacy, enlightenment, music, and the visual arts.

I joined the Communist Party while serving in the Soviet army as a young man. At a more mature age, I read the Bible and the Koran and discovered that socialist ethics and religious ethics have many things in common.

The Orthodox Church, by tradition, occupies a special place in the history of Russia. More than once, our statehood has been reborn thanks to its support. The renovated Communist Party of Russia has rejected atheism as a condition of membership.

A politician cannot understand Russia if he does not understand the central role of religion in the process of developing and establishing our statehood and culture. Such a politician would not be able to lead our country. By baptizing Russia a millennium ago, the grand prince

St. Vladimir laid the foundation of our unity. Without this, Rus would not have overcome the Tatar invasion or survived the Time of Troubles. During the Great Patriotic War, the Orthodox Church called upon the people to defend our native land. All our chronicles, historical works, and spiritual music originated in the monasteries.

On Culture

If art calls for kindness, justice, freedom, and beauty as it lifts one's spirits—this is the highest kind of politics. And for our people the question of freedom and justice is eternal. Art serves these goals. But freedom without justice equals social Darwinism, when predators devour all others, just as justice without freedom can lead to a brutal leveling in which different talents are forced to fit a single mold. Artists must be free, but they also must be patriotic. I do not believe that an artist can remain outside politics when Russia is on the edge of an abyss.

Literature in Russia has never been apolitical. If a writer gets tired of being responsible for the world, he capitulates and betrays his calling. This is what the current crisis in Russia is all about. In Russia, literature has always been more important than it has in Europe.

Without financial protection, our native culture will yield to a commercial and implanted Western culture. Our ballet, opera, and films are being pushed out of the world's art arena. Without correcting this, we could gradually deprive ourselves of our historical-cultural foundations.

Commercialization of real art is impossible. Only mass culture can be financially profitable. Basic science, the arts, museums, theaters, libraries, and other creative organizations must be partly or totally supported by the state.

Television is today the most important channel for influencing minds, but it is currently pouring out a stream of vulgarities promoting contempt for culture. We are shown three main scenarios: money and money games, endless murders and violence, and pornography. I am in favor of setting up a public council for television consisting of noted scholars, educators, writers, and priests.

The worst kinds of Western products of culture are being brought into our society on a mass scale. The commercialization of our culture degrades and reduces the national cultural space and creates inside

Russian society an atmosphere in which the person with more money, more capital, sets the tone.

We face a progressive "Americanization" of our culture, which is already dangerously deprived of national spirit. Most of our movie theaters show American films, predominantly containing pornography and violence.

The current rulers have eliminated the state financing of our culture. Expenditures on culture comprise 0.3–0.4 percent of the annual budget. Our national publishing business is close to bankruptcy.

About History

Even in the Soviet era, I never agreed that we had no history before 1917. I did not agree with the motto "We all were born in October." And, by the same token now, I do not agree that we had a period of anti-history. History and culture should be treated as continuing entities, the bridges from one epoch to the next. You cannot start your life anew from some given day of your choice. The same is true about nations.

Our nation has one history. It should be studied rather than cursed. You cannot throw out Peter the Great, or Alexander the Third, who did so much for Russia, or Lenin, or Stalin.

We have one Russia, and all those who are ready to defend its interests should find their places here. But Russia's interests definitely include the interests of its history of the twentieth century and its culture of the twentieth century. All of it. If you do not respect the history of your fathers, your children, likewise, will treat you with contempt. The twentieth century has been a complicated epoch for Russia. We have had so much war, from the Russo-Japanese War [1904–5] to the Great Patriotic War [1941–45]. Each generation went through its own war. We started the century with a great tragedy, and we are close to finishing it with another. Our country is on the edge of an abyss. It is losing its uniqueness and becoming a semicolony. We must prevent this by all means possible.

If we look at our thousand-year-long history, it becomes clear that the moral-ethical principles of Orthodox Christianity and socialist ideas coincide in many respects. There have been two core tendencies that have shaped world development. One is private-egoistical, and the other is social-collectivistic. The private-egoistical tendency has been expressed variously through fascism and wars, between generations and across continents. At the beginning of our century, because of terrible social contradictions, revolutionary cataclysms shook Russia and other countries. In the fall of 1929, a crisis in America put millions out of work and onto the streets. Eventually, President Roosevelt gathered the fifty people who controlled all the capital in America and told them: "Give me 40 percent of your income, and I will use the money to create work programs for the unemployed, retrain those who can be helped, and change the profiles of our obsolete industrial plants. Otherwise, America will go the way of Russia in 1917." All of them agreed to give him the needed money. The essence of his reforms was to combine the harsh private-egoistical form with the socio-collective form of life. Without ever using the word, he socialized American life.

All of this is history from which we should learn.

On Science and Education

The antipeople regime is driving our country's science into an early grave. The reason for this is that foreign capital, which is out to get our natural wealth, can reach its goal only by first technologically enslaving Russia and destroying our science and advanced technologies. The humiliation of our national dignity and threats are used as instruments to put pressure on our scientific institutions. From time to time, small concessions and promises are made to force the current regime to cooperate in this process. This cooperation leads to further retreats on the part of our pro-Western leaders.

Everywhere else in the world, science, especially basic science, is supported by the government. Our current regime could not do this even if it wanted to, because Russia's state treasury is almost empty due to the negligent destruction of the production sector of our economy. Our country's science will improve only when the entire national economy of Russia improves. However, in the meantime, we must urgently adopt serious multilevel measures.

First, we should heed the advice of our scientists concerning the needed structural changes for an optimal allocation of resources to the Russian Academy of Sciences, universities, research institutes, and design bureaus.

Second, our unique institutions—academic and scientific "towns," scientific centers—all need to receive immediate assistance from the federal government and local authorities.

Third, our science has traditionally been supported by our own national system of education, which includes science schools renowned all over the world. This tradition must be continued without a break; otherwise we will face a dearth of teachers for the next generation of our young people.

We must save the scientific-technical potential of our country. We must prevent a "brain drain" due to the emigration of our best scientists. And we must act before it is too late.

About the West

We have only begun to understand how the West, while talking about Russia's "admission to civilization," has actually been trying to remove or weaken its chief geopolitical competitor. The West has always considered historical Russia—whether the Russian Empire or the Soviet Union—to be its number one geopolitical rival. Our territory has been subjected to so many intrusions and invasions because of Russia's unique proximity to all the power centers of America, Asia, and Europe.

As a rule, attempts to conquer us have been covered over by some ideological veneer. But in reality, all conquerors-to-be came to us for our land and our wealth, hoping ultimately also to enslave our souls and take away our faith.

After the Caribbean crisis, John Kennedy formulated a radically new doctrine aimed at Russia. It was not called perestroika or radical reform but was, in fact, a program for destroying the USSR from within. He gathered a small group of specialists and told them: "A military confrontation with the USSR would be fatal for us. We need an effective policy to undermine the USSR from the inside."

According to some sources, America made a $200 net profit on every Russian killed during World War II. By 1945, America owned 50 percent of the world's gold currency reserves.

But today, the West is not tightly unified. There are those who hate Russia and are ready to erase it from the face of the earth. But there are others (including business circles) who understand Russia's important role, its geopolitical place in the world, and its importance in maintaining a balance in the huge expanse of Eurasia. They are ready to cooperate with us. We should respond reciprocally, assuring them that we can and will create normal conditions for their work in Russia and that we will insure their investments and guarantee their legitimate profits. But this must be an honest cooperation of equal partners.

Not everyone in the West will accept us on equal terms. We are a communal nation, brought up on a thousand years of experience in mutual support and patriotic feeling. And the West is trying to impose on us their individualism and Protestant egotism. Some in the West would demand that we live by rules that are completely alien to us, which we could never accept.

Today, our people are beginning to understand the sophisticated forms that Western expansion takes on and are reacting with growing spiritual resistance. In spite of powerful propagandistic deception, our people are beginning to wake up and realize that they may be deprived of their Fatherland, their culture, their rights to perpetuate their families, and their opportunity to move freely in their own country. They see how talk about "developed capitalism" has produced a feudal-clan administrative system busily accumulating primary capital by the ruthless methods used in the West during the seventeenth and eighteenth centuries. They realize that to repeat those former stages of West European history would mean a catastrophic step back for Russia.

Some Europeans would like to see a Russia that is a barbarian country they could "civilize" in their own way; a large Russia they could subdivide; an aggressive Russia against which they could organize coalitions; a reactionary Russia with a decaying religion that could be subjected to a forced Reformation or a conversion to Catholicism; or an economically inefficient Russia possessing underused territory and unlimited raw materials, which these Europeans would like to claim for themselves or at least exploit.

A New Soviet Union?

Voluntary reunification is inevitable. It is a matter of common sense. Time will soon tell what form this reunification will take.

The document adopted by the Duma in March 1996[6] cannot physically or legally resurrect the USSR as it existed before December 1991. This is perfectly understood even by those who shout the loudest about the fragmentation of the USSR. But at the same time, it is also clear to everyone that there is a real need for a definitive political and moral assessment of the Belovezh Agreements (which had been undertaken behind the backs of the peoples of the USSR and against their will). Without such an assessment, it will be impossible to begin the reintegration of the post-Soviet realm.

The State Duma's document in no way encroaches on the sovereignty of the new members of the CIS [Commonwealth of Independent States]; its only purpose is to open a way for the orderly and voluntary reintegration of the fraternal peoples.

The general denunciation of the Belovezh Agreements came as no surprise. Beginning in 1993, the CPRF on numerous occasions stated the need to restore historical justice and confirm the results of the popular referendum calling for the preservation of the USSR.[7] During the past two years, this question has been put to vote in the Duma fourteen times—each time collecting more votes.

The denunciation of the Belovezh Agreements was well deserved. These agreements brought grief and suffering to all peoples and inflicted much damage to the economies and the security of the fraternal republics. Five years of disunion have demonstrated that no single republic can climb out of the crisis by itself. It is our political and moral right to abrogate these agreements. But this does not mean that tomorrow someone will forcibly be joined with someone else. No one is about to challenge someone else's sovereignty. The right to reunite belongs to the people and no one else. But we would take all necessary steps to reestablish (on a voluntary basis) fraternal ties among Russia, Ukraine, Belarus, and Kazakhstan. This would start the incremental voluntary reestablishment of a federal union state.

On Nuclear Safety

There have been sustained efforts to create the impression that Russia as a nuclear nation is irresponsible. Russia itself is being led to believe that it has a political inferiority complex that makes it a dangerous country. Insidiously, the rationale for establishing an international tutelage over Russia is being created. This threatens to undermine and erode our national security.

The problem of safekeeping nuclear substances and controlling their proliferation has assumed great importance. There have certainly been cases of illegal dissemination of these substances in practically all parts of the world, including Western Europe and the United States.

We are for international cooperation in ensuring nuclear safety, which is equally important for us all. But in some important areas involving Russia's security—areas concerned with the storage and control of nuclear materials—our country is gradually losing its sovereignty through growing dependence on the "assistance" of other countries and the international organizations these countries control.

What do you think prevents the carrying out of the various schemes and projects aimed against our country's interests? And there are more of these plots now than during the Soviet era. One of the main factors cooling down hostile intentions is Russia's strategic nuclear arsenal—or, to be more exact, what is still left of it (the part not destroyed by Gorbachev and Yeltsin).

Armed Forces

We are against saber rattling, against the assumption by any state of the posture of a self-appointed international gendarme, against the eastward expansion of NATO. We are for peace. But it is unwise to beg for peace on your knees. Our armed forces must receive all they need for the secure defense of Russia's borders in the interests of peace.

Our army needs to be reformed. This applies equally to organizational and military-technical aspects and to the ideological-moral state of all members of the armed forces. A strong army must love its Fatherland, have confidence in its leaders, and be socially protected. Our country needs a military doctrine that guarantees our national security and makes it illegal to use the armed forces against the people.

A statesman once said, "If you are unwilling to keep and feed your own army, you will soon feed someone's else army." This is very much to the point! Look how eagerly NATO is trying to move closer to our borders, cutting our country off from its natural allies, partners, and markets. This development is synchronized with the destruction of our defense industry, armed forces, national self-awareness, and spirituality.

We must take off our hats and bow our heads before Russia's officers, sailors, and soldiers, who have selflessly protected our humiliated Fatherland and defended the armed forces from complete collapse.

Kremlin Plots

In March 1996, there was an [aborted] attempt to make a power play. The pretext was the Duma's denunciation of the Belovezh Agreements. The Duma resolution, which had been expected for a long time, suddenly provoked hysteria. I want to remind you that since 1993 the CPRF had repeatedly stated that it was necessary to restore historical justice and confirm the results of the March 1991 referendum calling for the preservation of the USSR. During the first two years of the First Duma, this question was put to a vote fourteen times. In December 1995, it mustered 209 votes, just short of the number needed to adopt a resolution. At that time, no one fell into a rage. But now, before the presidential elections, the authorities are trying to grab at what they believe is a suitable pretext to cancel the elections.

* * *

Today we know enough to state that in December 1993 the Constitution was adopted as the result of a fraudulent addition of nine million ballots to the tally. This fact was confirmed by the published results of an American electronic-intelligence data survey which has not been challenged by the central authorities nor by the Election Commission. Unfortunately this can no longer be checked because all the documents have been destroyed.

* * *

During the last week of June 1996—between the two rounds of the presidential elections—Boris Yeltsin suffered a heart attack. This fact was concealed from the Russian people, the State Duma, and the Central Electoral Commission. In a matter of days, this deception by omission became a lie by commission when Yeltsin's top aides officially assured the public that their boss was merely indisposed by a mild case of laryngitis. Voters who cast their ballots on July 3 for the next president of Russia were unaware of the true state of Yeltsin's health. There is no doubt in my mind that, had the voters known the truth, the results of the second round of the presidential elections would have been different, and Russia could have been spared weeks of agonizing confusion, uncertainty, and embarrassment.

"Junior Partner"? No Way.

This piece originally appeared in The New York Times
on February 1, 1996.

It is often said in the American press that Russia's Communists are by definition unfriendly to reform and to the United States. Yet the Communist Party of the Russian Federation was born six years ago precisely as a party of reform in opposition to decades of stagnation and to Mikhail Gorbachev's itch for revolution. While the West sang hallelujahs to perestroika, we knew that revolutions in Russia have always had painful consequences.

We thus called for evolutionary reform consistent with Russian historical traditions and world trends. Unfortunately, we were not listened to, and the Soviet Union collapsed.

Boris Yeltsin's regime has thoughtlessly tried to bring the "blessings" of neoliberalism to Russia, whose economy and character are quite different from those in the West. The results have been disastrous: The gross domestic product and living standards have fallen drastically. Mr. Yeltsin's promises to increase social spending and improve living conditions are merely an electoral maneuver.

Mr. Gorbachev and Mr. Yeltsin are considered friends of the United States. Although we are denied this honor, we will share with you our view on post-Yeltsin relations between the United States and Russia and of Russian foreign policy.

We would restore the might of the Russian state and its status in the world. That would make its policies incomparably more predictable and responsible than they are today.

Our foreign-policy priority would be to maintain continuity with the foreign policies of prerevolutionary Russia and the Soviet Union. We would seek to restore our state's unique role as the pivot and fulcrum of a Eurasian continental bloc—and its consequent role as a necessary balance between East and West.

We consider the disruption of military and strategic parity caused by the collapse of the Soviet Union dangerously destabilizing. And we see the restoration of the union of the former Soviet peoples—based on voluntary association—as a historical necessity dictated by Russia's needs and those of world security. Guided by pragmatism, we would free foreign policy of ideology, which imposes ruinous actions and obligations. We reject fantasies about "world revolution" but also consider the "new world order" no less alien to Russian interests. And we would stringently adhere to universal moral principles and the norms of international law.

Above all, we would concentrate on internal healing and national rebirth. The foreign policy conducive to this effort would be limited to maintaining state security. This rules out being drawn into supranational organizations that claim the right to interfere in others' internal affairs. Thus, we take an extremely negative view of plans to expand NATO into Eastern Europe, up to Russia's border, and we regard the entry of NATO troops into the former Yugoslavia as the first step toward carrying out those dangerous plans.

Several years have passed since the cold war ended, but relations between our countries are far from harmonious. Though it must renounce useless and excessive military spending, Russia never was—or could be—a "junior partner." For Americans, too, the burden of being the only superpower is unnecessary and undesirable. Any policy that counts on Russia's remaining in its humiliating position, following in the American wake, is doomed to defeat.

We respect our democratic traditions and outstanding achievements. We are deeply interested in expanding economic cooperation and educational, scientific, and cultural exchanges. We are ready to guarantee American investments and to create better conditions for them than now exist.

Recognizing the uniqueness of the American experience, we insist on acknowledgment of our equal right to follow our own path in accordance with our traditions and conditions. The principle of diversity, on which you have successfully based your domestic policy, should extend to foreign policy as well.

Editor's Notes

1. All other union republics comprising the Soviet Union had their separate communist parties. The largest republic, Russia, was an exception until a Communist Party of Russia was established in 1990.

2. During the early 1980s, *mujahedeen* began to infiltrate Tajikistan from neighboring Afghanistan, where Soviet troops were defending the pro-Soviet regime.

3. Much of Georgia was put under a Russian protectorate in 1783. For three centuries prior to that, Georgia was subjected to several partitions between Iran and Turkey.

4. Alexander N. Yakovlev was Gorbachev's closest associate during the years of perestroika. After the collapse of the Soviet Union at the end of 1991, Yakovlev became a senior adviser to Boris Yeltsin.

5. With the appointment of Yegor Gaidar as Yeltsin's acting prime minister. Gaidar served in the Russian government in various capacities from November 1991 to January 1994.

6. This was the communist-sponsored denunciation of the agreement dissolving the Soviet Union that had been reached by the presidents of the Russian, Ukrainian, and Belarusian union republics in December 1991 at a hunting lodge in the Belovezh Forest (near Minsk). The three presidents who signed the agreement were Boris Yeltsin (Russia), Leonid Kravchuk (Ukraine), and Stanislav Shushkevich (Belarus).

7. By a majority of about two-thirds, participants in the referendum voted on March 17, 1991, to preserve the union.

Part 2

The Drama of Power

From Perestroika to Catastrophe

The articles comprising Zyuganov's book The Drama of Power *(1993) were written and published in various Russian periodicals during the early 1990s, when the Soviet Union either was still in existence or had just collapsed and when the real political power in Moscow was moving from Mikhail Gorbachev to Boris Yeltsin.*

Presented here are selected parts of this compendium, mostly entire sections but in a few instances condensations or excerpts from some of the longer or more dated articles.

—V.M.

Three Times

To the terms that define our time, such as "perestroika," "democratization," and "glasnost," a new one was added recently—"crisis." The
wounds from national conflicts are bleeding, shop shelves are being
emptied, and aggressiveness is growing in practically every group of
people. This crisis manifests itself in many unexpected ways; today its
most frightening aspects are twofold: the shortage of competence and
the feebleness of political will.

By now, almost everyone can see that the "foremen" of perestroika
are trying to erect a state edifice whose joints will not fit and whose
corners will not fall into place. The construction project is governed
not by normal team discipline but by the principle of indiscriminate
sovereignty, which seems to mean that lower administrative units are
equal to or greater in authority than higher administrative units.

No social or biological system lives and works by this principle
anywhere in the world. But in theory, a system in which a village chief
can cancel any decision of a prime minister is not new. Anarchism has
left its mark in our history, but it seems that we do not learn from the
past. Hence, we have the following results: an economy that is becoming more and more disorganized, and historical ties that are becoming
weaker day by day. The population is disappointed and depressed, and
indifference and irresponsibility dominate public attitudes. People are
panicking: some are leaving the Party, and some are leaving the country. But those at the top are bluntly pretending that nothing unusual is
happening.

The masses have gradually come to understand that perestroika is a
difficult and delicate task, not an endless talk mill, and that we have
gone far enough to destabilize our society. The cavalry charges and
horse-driven carts with mounted machine guns used in 1917 are different in effect from the nuclear reactors and missile submarines of today.
The latter can, alas, in a few moments obliterate any legal differences
between a constitutional monarchy and a democratic confederation.

What we need are coordinated and purposefully designed systemic
transformations rather than acts of irresponsible destruction. The wise
Rasul Gamsatov [a Dagestani poet] remarked that a new Sweden cannot be created in Dagestan, just as the Swedes, despite their devotion
to hard work, cannot create a new Dagestan in their country. World
civilization, to which we "lost lambs" are supposed to return, consists

not only of a West European lifestyle and North American comfort but also of the multifaceted Latin America, boiling Africa, and the economic miracles of Asia. And, finally, it is also the difficult evolution of "Homo Sovieticus," designed not by some arrogant mind but rather through our history, rich both in tragedy and in surges of liberated spirit.

How we hoped that glasnost, this beloved child of perestroika, would grow into a beautiful precursor of true justice! We hoped that stagnation would evaporate, repressive barriers would fall, while good will and mutual human trust would blossom and fraternal interests and the national desire to put in order our common home would rise. How difficult to see instead before your eyes an ugly creature with a narrow forehead, a malicious look, and a screaming voice laughing heartlessly at the bedside of her own sick Motherland.

I beg my readers to understand that I am not given to emotional reactions. But under glasnost today the splendid intentions of a spiritual liberation and cleansing of society are often distorted beyond recognition, to the point of threatening the national health of the people and the entire cause of perestroika.

The spoken and written word has always been more essential in Russia than anywhere else. For a long time there was no legal means of opposition in our country. Some opposition was voiced by daring writers, whose talent and conscience stemmed from the people and who could feel their pain and expectations. But today's prophets and leaders are in reality frauds. They do not care about the people and their needs. They have appropriated the press, radio, and television and are holding the people hostage to their borrowed opinions and distorted tastes. The official monopoly on truth has been replaced by a new monopoly, now by gang members who are just as intolerant of different opinions. The very same people who so recently preached the "absolute truth" of "advanced socialism," cried hallelujah, crawled before their superiors, and supported any initiatives from above without regard to common sense now furiously and fervently worship new gods and spread different ideas. Could it be that they have "seen the light"? Everything is possible. But prejudice, anger, and nihilism are poor guides in the search for true values.

A cure sometimes requires bitter medicine. But what if the cure is worse than the disease? Glasnost has become a kind of psychological warfare against our own people. To promote further destabilization, rumors are concocted and circulated, criminal activities are justified, generations are set against each other, and the army and the people are depicted as adversaries. Sophisticated technological methods are used to portray whole republics, parties, and social groups as enemies. Mass-media reports about prisons and coffin factories, the cruelty of tyrants and the privileges of the "elite," and deprivation and hardships are designed to provoke more lawlessness and create a greater thirst for destruction and pillage.

All these things have happened before. Our country lived through the suppression of private entrepreneurs, the destruction of churches and manor houses, the repression of the intelligentsia, the demolition of sacred relics, and the denunciation of entire nations as enemies. While we rehabilitate and repent, we simultaneously create new enemies. Look at the newspapers of the 1930s. Are not some of the arguments used then identical to the intolerant and provocative statements now being made?

In the past, people designated as undesirables were hunted down by men with weapons in their hands. Today, modern headhunters follow their prey with telecameras and tape recorders. They interrogate neighbors, relatives, and acquaintances to dig up "dirt." They sit for days to ambush unsuspecting victims in unflattering positions. Experts in sexual pathology have suddenly switched to producing political portraits so humiliating that ideologists of the Third Reich could not have done better—or worse. And this is happening after the publication of the Law "On the Print Media."

An American author, Sam Keen, wrote a curious book a few years back entitled *Faces of the Enemy*.[1] Later a movie was made from this book. He very convincingly showed how each great crime against humanity is preceded by a campaign of hatred that transforms the enemy into a subhuman who is nobody's son, brother, or father and who can be killed without any pity. This demonization happened in Europe before the beginning of World War II; in Japan before the attack on Pearl Harbor; and in the United States before the first atomic bomb was dropped on Hiroshima—and also when badges appeared saying "Kill a Russian" during the cold war.

Today, we are assured that nothing similar is possible, that the authorities would never allow it to happen, and that we are building a humane law-based state. Well, as the saying goes, God is merciful! Or perhaps we will be let down again by the desire to destroy everything down to the ground first and begin a new life from next Monday? As you know, we recently witnessed extreme vandalism, but our authorities appear paralyzed. In fact, they are not very authoritative and resemble "clouds in trousers."[2] An infinite hot shower of laws, decrees, and orders, which nobody obeys, is pouring down upon us.

A kind of pseudoglasnost continues to permeate the country. It is part of a servile effort to implement a plan drafted decades ago by transatlantic experts: depict the Soviet Union as the largest and most predatory empire on earth, trivialize its heroes, demoralize its population, and revive national-religious schisms. This is probably the only "plan" that will be carried out during the current five-year-plan period.

Preliminary results are already visible. State television studios are being seized by mobs, state radio stations are transmitting calls for civil disobedience, and government officials are promoting general strikes. Monuments are being toppled, people who dare to carry red flags on "national" holidays are being beaten, undesirable journalists are being harassed, medals are being torn from veterans, trains are being stopped at will, and planes are being hijacked. And the people who are perpetrating these outrages are not Munich shopkeepers or Chicago gangsters but our own, domestically grown "fighters for perestroika." And they are being encouraged by opportunistic politicians.

Now we know what our late dictator was thinking some fifty years ago as he looked significantly at his colleagues. We have condemned the secret prewar protocols.[3] But we are at a loss when it comes to seeing how we can convert to a regulated market when none of the regulators is working. We are completely ignorant of what extreme measures should be put in place to fight rampant crime and of what responsible persons think of the fact that thousands of people who ride trains are suddenly unable to reach their homes, workplaces, or resorts and that in hundreds of instances products and goods are left out in the open to be ruined by the elements or pilfered. In any democratic country, such things are referred to simply and clearly as terrorism. And this brings appropriate consequences for those who break the laws. We, however, prefer a different explanation: these are our civic activists asserting their freedom by taking over stations and having fun with railroad lines.

Today, our glasnost regime is not only suffering from social color-blindness but is also careless and indifferent to everyday problems. It has almost forgotten the schoolchildren who lack boots, notebooks, and textbooks. It does not deign to notice today's refugees or the victims of crime or our unemployed youth. It is not concerned with such things as crop harvesting and preparations for the winter. It has started talking about the peasants but only after the peasants presented an ultimatum to the cities. In the meantime, in some cities bread rationing has reappeared; in others, residents receive less than the war-time quota of cereal grain. But in the nearby countryside, unprecedentedly high yields of crops cannot be harvested because nobody cares to help.

If glasnost fails to wake up the public, which has talked itself to sleep, we may face really big troubles. Glasnost encourages people to think that talking, and especially complaining, takes care of things. This is reminiscent of a character in the Saltykov-Shchedrin story who, upon returning from the vegetable garden, indignantly tells his wife: "Sweetheart, something strange is happening in our Fatherland. I've expressed my anger about three times, but the turnip still isn't growing."[4] Now our turnips and other goods have grown, but nobody wants to harvest them. Some of our citizens are going abroad, some are canoeing, while our markets offer only rotten cabbages and half-grown carrots. And everybody is silent.

These days glasnost is creating new "idols." Among them are a hard-luck associate professor, a talkative builder, a reprimanded general, and a noted historian without notable publications. They are characters of a different caliber. Many are sleek rascals, professional squabblers, pimps, and prostitutes. Completely missing from the list are real creators of new life, such as Likhachev, Paton, Fyodorov, Kabaidze, or Starodubtsev.[5] Their place has been taken by the members of a striptease group called "Pioneers of Sex-Grave Erotica" who perform in open city squares and sports arenas where your typical spectator is a fan aged 13–17. Isn't this just like a "feast during the plague"?[6] Any state that promotes the moral corrosion of its children and cannot ensure the inviolability of the home may be considered criminal and has lost any right to collect taxes or call itself a state.

Recently, I opened one of our magazines. Inside, I found the promising heading of a new section—"People." At last, I expected to see articles about men like the Russians who in eighteen months built a car factory on the Volga; or like our young Ural engineers in the Great Patriotic War who in forty days designed, built, and produced tanks that stood up to the "Tigers" and "Ferdinands";[7] or perhaps like those men who, led by Korolyov, created a new rocket system each year.[8]

There was nothing of that sort. The pages of the magazine were, as usual, adorned with gloomy portraits of notorious historical villains. Among them was the Roman emperor Nero. The story was well written, curdling one's blood. But the article did not explain what made him a murderous tyrant. It did not describe how he became the first poet of the empire by hiring a few scores of claqueurs. And when this crazy poet could not create a scene of fire in his poem, he ordered a torch put to Rome, hoping to be inspired by the sight of a burning city.

The word "perestroika" connotes "building," not "enflaming." Glasnost stands for the search for truth, not terrorism and outrages committed upon everything that is holy. Democracy means the people's power, not anarchy. Anarchy, like dictatorship, leads to the atrophy of conscience followed by asphyxia and ultimately the decomposition of the whole social organism.

Truth Requires Courage and Will

Marx observed that social consciousness most intensively decays in two seemingly mutually exclusive cases: when the people see a crime but see no punishment for it; and, on the contrary, when they see the punishment but do not know the alleged crime.

Our country endured a period when people saw punishments abound—neighbors and comrades disappeared—but they did not know the reason. Today, we seem determined to prove the validity of the second part of Marx's paradox. Submarines are sinking; trains are being blown up; the *chernozem* [black earth]—a centimeter's layer of which requires 100 years to form—is being sold. In a matter of hours, 200 kilometers of the state border, sacred and inviolable, are removed. Various emissaries travel throughout the country instigating violence of one people against another.

No one is blamed for this except the insignificant "scapegoats." Nor is there an appropriate reaction by the public. Justice is silent and so is the Supreme Soviet. In our glasnost age, responsibility has become anonymous. It is now more difficult to identify malefactors who are alive than to blame our malaise on those who have died. Irresponsible acts continue, while the country desperately needs stable working conditions and law and order.

Power has always been the main prize of any revolution. Today, everyone speaks about it: the left and the right, centrists and born-again monarchists, desperate radicals and typical conservatives—even those who have never been involved in politics. "All Power to the Soviets," "Down with the Power of the Party Bosses," "Apparatchiks Have Grabbed Power," "Party, Give Us the Steering Wheel"—the din of these slogans continues by force of inertia. But if a group has seized power, why are the leading experts so alarmingly complaining about a "vacuum of authority," "powerlessness," and "paralysis"? This is because many of us have again become victims of one more manipulation of social consciousness. The fact that all of the thirty or so laws adopted in one year by the Supreme Soviet do not work properly makes people think: What is the matter? The matter is simple enough. For any law to function, at a minimum two conditions must be met: there must be a mechanism that makes the law work, and the law has become part of the general consciousness. Given these conditions, one consciously avoids stepping over the line that is forbidden by law.

Party power strongly built into the mechanism of administrative management had long been a feature of the state system. While the Party often usurped and even abused administrative authority, it also cemented the whole public organism. Although it was natural to remove the Party from the administrative mechanism, this expulsion was done so abruptly that the administration shuddered to a stop. This breakdown has created a dangerous situation—and not only for us. Our country has all kinds of weapons and should not be left without a reliable control system. Unfortunately, once again we destroyed the old system in haste, and now, in equal haste, we are trying to create something new. We leap first and think later.

Today we attach much hope to the presidential office, believing that it can restore the normal functioning of the state. However, a reconstructed executive branch would be able to solve our problems only if it were firmly supported. Our Party has much to do through individual communists who work in all bodies of power. But now this should be done in different ways and by different methods.

What actions are needed to change the situation for the better? In my opinion the answer is clear. We need to ensure the preservation and consolidation of a unified Soviet Union on the basis of a renewed federation. We need to accelerate the resolution of urgent problems within Russia—the core of the Union. We need uniform laws and rules of human community for all the peoples living in our country. We need a uniform and consolidated Communist Party. And we need to maintain reliable defenses.

Crime is the strongest destructive factor in our situation. Increased crime is the main negative result of all our miscalculations. Crime is rampant, the statistics are overwhelming, the press is having a field day, and the man in the street is terrified but is lapping it all up. I might add that this situation is actually worse than it seems at first glance. In 1989, for example, almost 45,000 more people lost their lives to crime in one way or another than in the previous year, and 109,000 more people were robbed, maimed, or raped than in the year before. Ponder these figures. They are greater than our losses in the ten-year Afghanistan war. Remember that our people in Afghanistan were soldiers carrying out orders. That is some consolation. And what about now, here in Russia?

There is a lot of shouting about the red and white terror. But doesn't all this talk push us once again into settling old bloody accounts? The country is (as many years ago) witnessing pogroms, arsons, refugees. In the past three years, there have been almost 30 attempted cases of airplane hijackings and about 700 averted attempts. In the meantime, the tidal wave of mass street meetings threatens to sink our loosely built ship of state. National conflicts are raging across the entire country, but hardly anyone has been punished for instigating them. Why does this occur? What promotes it? What measures should be taken? Who is responsible?

Almost all public institutions have made some contributions to the continuing growth of crime. And if we do not admit this, no special police forces, truncheons, or armored vests will be enough. We must all accept responsibility.

Look at the products of our mass culture, which now is dominated by the cult of an idle life, sex, and vulgarity. Yet our renowned cultural leaders, for reasons unknown, are silent. They are now so busy in the political arena that they have no time for anything else. Take, for example, our cinematography. Members of this industry were in the first rank of perestroika advocates. But recently, they have been flooding the screens of our movie theaters with pictures showing naked men and women. Recall the past five or six years of our films for the young, during which a fully justifiable protest against social problems has been repeatedly expressed by primitive scenes of brutal sexual violence against women. Why then should we be surprised that such brutal crimes as rape have been mushrooming?

When a pleasant commentator with a "robotized" voice tells millions of television viewers, without a trace of protest or compassion, about dismembered corpses and children dumped from bridges or found in trash dumps, this is more than the dissemination of information. It is ethical anesthesia, which lowers the moral standards of society and legitimizes indifference and permissiveness. Psychologists know this very well. But try to object, and you will be attacked from all sides. However, if we wish to live in normal human conditions, we will have to take these problems seriously and correct them.

The highest principle of education is devotion to truth. As Pushkin said, where there is truth, beauty will appear by itself. But truth requires courage, will, and the ability to analyze. Unfortunately, truth itself often becomes an object of speculation and is mixed with conjecture and self-interest. As a result, while fighting dogmatism we often end up engaging in neodogmatism ourselves. Examples of this are numerous.

Bringing this principle to a practical level, let us look at the administrative-command system. A lot of money has been made by cursing and damning it. It is clear even for someone who is not initiated in its intricacies that this system can be overcome only by introducing a more modern system, one that is better organized and more efficient. It is also true that some administrative abuse is inevitable as long as we have a shortage of culture, knowledge, and conviction. So let us upgrade the level of our professionalism and culture rather than concentrating on finding a "magic system." Much should be done in this area. We should also realize that legality and the law require consistent administrative enforcement, especially in a country with an out-of-balance economy. We need to find the proper proportion for the use of administrative enforcement while striving to switch, as soon as possible, to effective economic methods.

A legitimate desire for self-reliance has been equated with absolute independence and freedom, which do not exist in nature. Nor are we likely to invent them, though we love to claim we are doing something "for the first time ever." This tendency leads to a separatism that is tearing apart the living fabric of our country, the republics, the territories, branches of the economy, nations, and even families. Others have decided that independence means "do it your own way." This philosophy leads to situations where many Party [CPSU] committees with newly elected members simply have ceased to function.

How are we supposed to take the frequent assertion that the mass media merely reflect life? This makes journalists to be no more than messengers, not responsible for the message. In reality, the media not only reflect but have long been organizing, forming, imposing, persuading, directing, and manipulating. If this were not so, why would anybody pay huge sums for commercial advertising, conceal new technologies, or seek editorial posts? The media's power to influence has existed for a long time. But now this power can be bought not only in rubles but also in dollars. Whoever controls the stock of the media outlets dictates his own terms and controls access to information.

The power of the mass media was particularly evident during the last elections. Five members of the small editorial staff of the weekly magazine *Arguments and Facts* were elected people's deputies. I do not question their electoral mandates or personal qualities. But I am concerned that their media importance may have been too easily converted to political authority. This is indeed a phenomenon that apparently has never occurred before in the history of our country or, for that matter, of any other country. It can be safely entered in the *Guinness Book of World Records*.

We should allow no further abuses of the power of information. Otherwise we will be given a new "off-limits" zone for criticism, a new "*okhranka*" that may not be any better than the previous one.[9] We should remember that deliberately targeted information can create a powerful sensation of imminent violence—a psychotic state that can compel people to arm themselves even if they have never held weapons in their hands before.

Neodogmatism has been used in most sophisticated ways in the fight against apparatchiks.[10] The current campaign against them has exceeded similar efforts undertaken during the 1920s. The central Party apparatus is portrayed as the source of all our problems. Such wholesale condemnation of the apparatus is convenient for some people today—those who hold power but fail to make timely decisions and then hide behind the muzzled apparatus, those who are afraid to criticize their superiors by name but who are willing to attack anonymous members of the apparatus, and those who do not see the real reasons for our difficulties and use members of the apparatus as scapegoats. And there are also those who crave power themselves and have already secretly prepared their own new apparatuses.

I have never met a [Party] instructor who would pretend to be the secretary of a district, city, or regional Party committee.[11] But secretaries of Party committees cannot be considered apparatchiks. They are elected officials accountable to their committees. Today's critics of the Party, however, lump all together. We are dealing here with deliberate attempts to confuse different concepts with the intention of weakening and destroying the Party.

Perestroika's extremist enthusiasts have suggested that all Party officials, or perhaps the whole Party, should be deemed a collective enemy. They justify this on the basis of formal logic: all communists are in charge of something, hence they are all bureaucrats, and, therefore, they are all enemies. But if we took this as fact we would have to conclude that one out of every three or four people living in this country is an "enemy." The purges of 1937 would look like just a warm-up for an even greater cataclysm. This is a philosophical and moral impasse from which there is no way out for anybody. Unfortunately, our society is being pushed in this direction.

Lenin's memory is no longer spared from verbal attacks. For some renegades in our own country, Lenin has always been an impediment, because his powerful mind encompassed the whole world and injustice above all. This man, who could speak most of the European languages and who wrote fifty-five books in the fifty-four years of his life, continues to be one of the most read authors in the world. He was always distinguished by clarity of interpretation and awareness of the implications of various political viewpoints. He could anticipate the development of events and led the people accordingly. Our "nouveaux riches" are afraid of him because he always denounced cheats as parasites on the nation's body and warned that any relaxation of the struggle against them would be a crime against socialism.

Demagogues and intriguers fear Lenin because he saw through their deceptions. He warned that people will be victims of deception in politics until they learn to see the interests behind flowery words and phrases.

Let us remember this: There are no desperate situations, only desperate people. In any situation, it is possible to apply personal conscience and a sense of proportion. I have had to analyze various emergency situations. Some of these might never have occurred if the people involved in them had had a stronger sense of civic duty and personal responsibility.

The late Academician Legasov, who spent more time in Chernobyl than anyone else, said that the main reason for the disaster at the power plant was the fact that the engineers and technicians who managed it had to rely on their superiors—technocrats just like themselves—rather than on Tolstoy and Dostoevsky. Their moral and cultural levels were not adequate to make the decision required by the complexity of the technology entrusted to them. I think this is the basic reason for many other disasters in our country, which are also a matter of culture: the culture of management, the culture of mutual relations, the culture of analysis.

Where is the high level of our culture of analysis when we enrage television viewers by showing them lines of railroad cars waiting in vain to be unloaded even though each car has an earmarked destination and a specific person responsible for its timely delivery? If the TV cameras were to be redirected onto the idle bureaucrats, you would get goods to waiting consumers in no time.

To stabilize the situation in our country, we must change the tone of our printed and spoken words. Otherwise we will be at each other's throats. Our descendants will never forgive us for that. There is too much confrontation and dispute. We all remember what happened during the recent controversy over so-called promising versus unpromising villages.[12] It should be clear to everyone how counterproductive such arguments are. Yet new and no less destructive confrontations are pitting Russians against non-Russians, indigenous peoples against nonindigenous peoples, occupants against nonoccupants, emigrants against nonemigrants, supervisors against subordinates, and young against old. All this destroys our respect for traditions and continuity, although it is clear that no society can develop without these moral precepts.

We should, and will, overcome challenges with honor. No matter what anyone says, we will continue to believe in values such as Motherland, Fatherland, peace, home, family, love, freedom, labor, knowledge, justice, conscience, dignity, and charity. These values have been earned by the sufferings of humankind and affirmed by generations of our own ancestors. We must live up to this precious legacy.

With and Without Masks

By early 1991, the Yeltsin clique was moving to replace Gorbachev's team. It consolidated its ranks around a destructive policy, strength-

ened its social base, and stood ready to sweep aside anything in its path
... Even then it was clear that to achieve their purposes these circles
were ready to sacrifice the Soviet Union and Russia itself. I wrote an
article about this on the eve of the [March 17, 1991] referendum [on
preserving the Union].

On their way to power, the false democrats are prepared to sacrifice
all national and state interests. For the third time in this century, our
country is being dragged into a fratricidal conflict in which there can
be no victors. The surest path to this goal is the undermining and
destruction of the Soviet Union. It is no wonder that all such "democrats" are furiously opposed to the idea of a renewed Union of Sovereign Republics. But what a terrible price all the peoples of our country
would pay for a "divorce" conceived at the whim of politicians striving
to become "masters" and of the forces behind them!

The disintegration of the Soviet Union would prove to be a terrible
blow to the integrated economic organism of the country that took
centuries to develop. Here is just one example. Each one of 1,500
products vital both to the population and to the national economy is
being manufactured exclusively by only one factory for distribution
throughout the whole country. This is not the best situation, but this is
how it is. How can we deal with this problem if the Soviet Union
disintegrates?

The disintegration of the Soviet Union would inevitably result in
hundreds of thousands, even millions, of refugees and migrants. Let us
leave aside for the moment the moral and psychological aspects of this
problem and consider the economic aspect alone. World experience
has shown that a sum equivalent to 200,000 rubles is required to settle
one family of three or four people in a new place. When Boris Yeltsin
signed agreements with Estonia and Latvia that contained an article
about resolving the problem of migrants from the Baltic States to Russia, did he stipulate where the tens of billions of rubles for the recep-
tion of the migrants would come from? Even if only one out of ten
families living outside their "own" republic moved, more than a trillion
rubles would be required to resettle them. It would take even the most
healthy economy some twenty years to provide for this.

The disintegration of the Soviet Union could have unpredictable
consequences for the whole world. Such dissolutions do not occur
peacefully. Bloody conflicts inevitably occur, and a Lebanonization of
the country begins. Now imagine Lebanon or Karabakh as a country

that occupies one-sixth of the planet and is heavily armed with weapons of mass destruction. If we start to "throw stones" at each other, our neighbors will have broken glass in their windows or worse. The West, by the way, is beginning to realize this danger. But the same cannot be said of the "democratic forces." Otherwise, why would there be so much loose talk about creating a separate Russian army?

The Persian Gulf War demonstrated that the epoch of wars for natural resources is not over. Against this background, the attempt to dismember our economic and defensive potential shows a criminal indifference to the fate of millions and to the security of both present and future generations of our citizens. Who could guarantee that the regions of the Soviet Union rich in raw materials would not become arenas of armed confrontations between militarist groupings in the event of its disintegration?

During their most recent mass meeting in Moscow, the "democrats" asserted that they were for the Soviet Union but called for a vote "against" it in the March 17 referendum as an expression of no confidence in the president of the USSR and his government. Is it not insane to risk so much for the sake of so little? Even if we were to take this deception for sincere intentions, the outcome would be clear: the Soviet Union would cease to exist. Is this a rational way to express mistrust of some political figures and support for others? Of course, nothing will come of a scheme such as this. What do you take your own people for, forcing such actions upon them?

Our [Russian Communist Party] Plenum was right in stating that this is not about choosing between Gorbachev and Yeltsin, or about choosing a social system, but about the existence or the nonexistence of our country.[13]

At mass meetings on Manezh Square in Moscow and on Palace Square in Leningrad [in August 1991], the "democrats" Popov, Gdlyan, Starovoitova, Salye, and others proclaimed the entire CPSU to be a collective enemy of the people, thus condemning some 60 million Party members and their families.[14] After that, Otto Latsis of the newspaper *Izvestia* wrote an exposé entitled "Masks" that was aimed at the Plenum of the Central Committee of the Communist Party of Russia. The tone of the article differed little from the speeches on the two city squares. The street speakers talked about "traitors" and "gangsters," and he wrote about "enemies of perestroika" and "neo-Stalinists." Our friend, who spent much of his earlier career at the journal *Communist*, managed to misquote much of the Plenum's report. To be sure, this is nothing new for him.

Mr. Latsis, do you really not see that the country has lost its brakes and steering and is sliding ever more rapidly back into totalitarianism? Look at the Baltic States, republics to which you constantly gave advice. Basic human rights are already being routinely violated there. But you are silent about this. Take an unprejudiced look at "democratic" Georgia, where open genocide has been unleashed. Do we want this to happen in Russia?

Look at a report on crime and you will see that the number of civilian casualties of crime in our country in the past two years alone far exceeds our battle losses in the ten-year Afghan War. You apparently do not have enough courage to remove these masks. For you, Russia is apparently no more than an experimental laboratory, but we Russians are fed up with it.

The Fatherland Above All

We are talking about the Russian question not in its quasi-patriotic sense but in regard to its global historical significance. We are talking about the danger of losing a unique value—a strong state that for several centuries has acted as a guarantor of world stability. This would be a loss not only for our people but for all humankind. It is a fact of world history rather than an invention of the originators of the Russian idea that Russia has been a guardian—in the highest and most humane sense—of Europe and Asia and of the whole world. No other country could take its place.

The humiliating condition in which the citizens of a formerly great power find themselves disturbs their historical consciousness and, at the same time, awakens their national self-awareness. Intentional or not, the destruction of the state system will damage everybody's interests —workers, peasants, the intelligentsia, and businessmen. If the state falls, all will fall.

The paramount need for a union of state-patriotic forces has not yet been realized by all those who should be concerned. Among these diverse groups are state-oriented, genuine democrats who are aware of the danger of an Americanized presidency for the yet immature Soviet democracy; state-oriented patriots with a social consciousness and appreciation of Russian national pride; and state-oriented communists who accept the blame for having been too patient with the Party elite responsible for bringing the country to ruin and chaos.

To unite in one organization, they do not have to agree about all things, but they must be of a single mind about one thing—a genuine and deep sense of responsibility for the Russian-Soviet state and an understanding of the fact that this state is a historical form of the communal existence of the large and small peoples living in Russia, a form guaranteeing the civil rights about which so much is said and so little is actually done today.

We can anticipate a sarcastic remark: "You are attempting to unite things that oppose each other: democracy, the Russian idea, and socialism." History gives many examples of the unification of things that appear to be disparate when faced with the necessity of national survival. Who in 1933 would have thought that the United States, England, and France on the one hand and the USSR on the other—huge interests that seemed divided by an abyss of irreconcilable interests—would be united in an anti-Hitler coalition?

At present we are separated and splintered by ideological, political, and national hostilities and by our irreconcilably different views of history. When the anticommunist hurricane struck the country, many of us who sincerely longed for a purification thought that it was here. We failed to notice that the hurricane washed away the union's state structures, which certainly needed to be modernized but did not need to be liquidated.

The Commonwealth of Independent States offered to us today seems better than the Union of Sovereign States, which is a very unclear and amorphous form.[15] But the benefits promised by the Commonwealth—the development of economic relations on the basis of a single monetary unit, the ruble; the preservation of a unified command; control over nuclear weapons; and open state borders—have no guarantees of permanence. The benefits have survived, so far, thanks only to the unity of three state leaders in their opposition to the so-called Novo-Ogarevo formula "8 + 1." But the "+ 1" [the USSR] will soon become history. Then many problems will reappear, but they will be problems between states rather than between republics.

Our country, which paid the highest price for peace in World War II, has suffered a defeat forty-six years later at the hands of its own leadership. "But now we have freedom," someone may say. Freedom of what? Of total privatization, auctions at which what was created by the labor of many becomes the property of a few? Freedom of price liberalization?

History cannot be deceived, and it is for this reason that we had to recognize private property. But history also teaches that private property without a sense of social responsibility brings the confrontations that have cost us dearly in the past. Out of despair caused by chaos and by wild anarchy, when the law of lawlessness strikes at the very fiber of our state organism, our people will be compelled to opt again for dictatorship.

Honest and thinking citizens have tried to convince others that we need a change in our national economy to ensure the unity and proportionality of state, collective, and private ownership, which would connect and reconcile "mine" and "ours." This is close to the philosophy of the NEP [the New Economic Policy of the early 1920s].[16]

Does NEP once again mean Lenin? Yes, because it was Lenin who offered a deideologized development of our national economy. NEP is the unfinished page in the history of Soviet Russia that may not be able to be copied but that does deserve to be studied. What is important is the methodology of NEP: a way of forming an economy that combines economic freedom with strong state authority, ensuring that this freedom does not exceed the limits of necessity. When properly exerted, the authority of the state makes sure that private property does not suppress state property and vice versa.

Above all we need unity, which is so hard to achieve. Those who are still trying to drag us into the common European home and deprive us of our own home are quick to accuse some people of Russophobia and others of national-socialism and apostasy from the ideals of freedom and democracy. Politically, everything is done according to the same old principle—divide and rule.

In the meantime, the last state structures in the sphere of production are being destroyed. The threat of the destruction of the stratum of professional managers—administrators and managers of large industrial, scientific, and agricultural enterprises and military experts—is real.

Only Russia can become the center of the revival of a new union destined by history. Russia has been assigned this role by the historical development of our state. If Russia is seen to be a strong, flexible, and truly democratic state, other nations will be attracted to it because of historical necessity and good will. The modern era does not remove the need for a suitable federal system for the political community of peoples and nations that have created a unified historical space.

History shows that Russia's honor has always been defended by patriotic movements of its peoples. This happened at the time of the great trials. And it will happen again. History will work for us if we work for history.

Failures of Perestroika

I know that today millions of my compatriots are asking themselves: What should an honest person do who is convinced that the socialist choice is correct? We all see that blind and furious gasps of hatred are freezing and destroying our home. Crisis events are unfolding everywhere literally every day. I am not even talking about the breakdown of economic ties, the sharp drop in production, and shortages. I am depressed by the general mood: our people have grown tired of political talk mills, uncertainties, intolerance, and hostility. The idea of brotherhood and justice is rapidly becoming worthless because of a general lack of responsibility and a cult of violence.

The living conditions of socially unprotected people are deteriorating. Spiritual emancipation is turning into loose behavior and a mood of all-permissiveness. Intoxication with this kind of freedom has sharply increased nihilism in all legal matters. Under the banner of pluralism, our society has been penetrated by zoological anti-Sovietism. Today's "friends of the people" are persistently pushing the perestroika processes into a counterrevolutionary direction. The actions of the new authorities in many places show not only that we have gone back to a dictatorial style dressed in democratic verbiage but that this time the administrative power is in the hands of much more incompetent, intolerant, and cruel individuals than ever before.

We are displaying a fatal obsession with conferences. Last year, our ministers, politicians, and managers spent almost 150 days each in various organizational meetings. Many of them also managed to spend two or three months on official business trips abroad. With this kind of work schedule, no one could manage even a perfectly functioning national economy.

In short, the current goals of perestroika have moved away from its original idea, and any point of view that does not coincide with that of perestroika's "foremen" is immediately subjected to ostracism. And yet, the truth about what is happening in our country is coming out. Perestroika's main purpose—to open up the potential of socialism by engaging all the creative forces of the people—has not been realized.

There were major miscalculations in planning, followed by an attempt to solve all problems at once by haphazardly changing and juggling priorities. The political reforms were started from the wrong end by promoting political pluralism from the outset rather than first democratizing and modernizing the Communist Party.

The Party machine had internal organizational weaknesses, as was shown in the most recent elections of central, regional, and local state authorities.

The public has been pressured into believing that the mass media are a mirror that faithfully reflects reality and not a powerful instrument for influencing minds and moods. It was not fully understood that external forces were interested in making sure that events should unfold in a particular way.

A great error was to destroy the all-union structures of public and state management and control simply because these were part of the old system. Under the pretext of a struggle against the administrative-command system, mainstays of law and order, economic activity, and security—all vital for every state—have been seriously damaged.

Taken together, this proves beyond any doubt that the whole perestroika reform faces a crisis brought about by lack of competence, an absence of political will, and a deficient sense of ethics on the part of the leadership at various administrative levels. The crisis could definitely have been avoided.

On the Outcome of Seven Tragic Years

Formally, all peoples of the USSR have supposedly acquired independence, sovereignty, and freedom. But simultaneously, the joy in people's eyes and the feeling of well-being in their homes have disappeared. Our people are sick and tired of contentions, conflicts, social problems, lies, and hypocrisy.

To understand why this is so, it is enough to watch our bluntly pro-Yakovlev and totally Americanized television, which reacts and comments in identical ways about magnificent official receptions in the Kremlin and bloody interethnic carnages. The state TV lives on taxpayers' money while doing its utmost to destroy our state. What could be more ridiculous?

Here, for example, is a typical information cocktail eagerly broadcast and rebroadcast within a few hours by three or four announcers pretending to be professional commentators, people's deputies, casual observers.

"One more bloody massacre in Dubossar . . . In Tver, people in a bread line rioted and stormed the bakery . . . There is no gasoline in half the country's airports . . . In our country we have the highest level of crime . . . No! Now Czechoslovakia has overtaken us by declaring all communists to be criminals. Havel unexpectedly helped us! Shevardnadze finally admits that famine, cold, plus street people make a hellish mix.[17] He should know. He has experienced all this firsthand in Georgia. And Popov is about to flee his post as mayor of Moscow. . . .

Only our two Nobel Prize winners appear undisturbed and consistent. Television pictures resurrect the tireless Andrei Sakharov fighting for human rights (for some reason no one cares to follow in his footsteps). And Mikhail Gorbachev, shown with his still hopeful [wife] Raisa Maksimovna, is seen enjoying some rock music and an academic choir.

A real madhouse. No serious analyses are offered, no reasons for events are given, no consequences or conclusions are presented. We are one stop away from the infamous Russian free-for-all riot. One watches and wonders: Where are the democratic human-rights activists? Why are they nowhere to be seen? Are they really content with the total fascization of the country?

But the "democrats" have trapped themselves in a web of their own lies. It is unreasonable to expect an objective estimation of our new reality from those who have made every effort to create universal disorder. These are the people for whom Darwin's laws do not exist. They are grimly holding on to the "feeding trough" and refusing to yield to more conscientious and fit individuals. But the time is approaching when everybody—regardless of political orientation, religion, or amount of capital—will have to face reality. Without an honest assessment of the situation we cannot climb out of this mire.

The main reason for our tragedy must be eliminated first. It was caused by the forced imposition of a prehistoric liberalism that totally ignored the foundations of our statehood, the multinational character of the people and their sociopsychological life. Both the "architects" and the "foremen" of perestroika have shown themselves to be outrageous neo-Trotskyites.

By now, it is probably obvious to all that this liberal model was made for Russia by special order. Only this model provided a blueprint for breaking up a great nuclear power into pieces that "world civilization" could swallow without fear of choking. And it has seemingly accomplished its purpose. The conspiracy seems to be working. But, as the saying goes, the day is not over yet. As for "world civilization," it is dominated not by liberal ideas but by a traditionally conservative concept that development must be based on strong state and national interests. The West does not practice what it preaches. All the advisers of Mikhail Sergeevich [Gorbachev] and Boris Nikolaevich [Yeltsin] are fully aware of this.

Even when the country is still in the process of being revived from taking the wrong medicine, the new government of Russia is planning to give it a dose of another imported remedy—shock therapy of the Polish kind. It is difficult to imagine a more pernicious treatment. Why not listen instead to those who have been saying for years that the only way to get out of this crisis is through the stabilization and growth of production, not the manipulation of prices and salaries? The key criterion for developing and selecting programs to be introduced into the economy should be creative potential.

Russia does not need a new round of failed liberalism. It needs sound pragmatism coordinated with our historically formed system of moral-ethical values. Russia is ready to accept a genuine market instead of market mirages. We need an economic environment with various forms of ownership. Our people have long since earned some well-deserved peace and rest. But this is hardly possible unless we convince them that no one will be saved one by one and that we must together develop and implement a well thought through program of national security.

Now the emotional state of our citizens can be described by one word—deception. This feeling of having been deceived is shared by those who sincerely believed we were close to a triumph of democracy and humanism and who hoped to live in a comfortable, prospering, and law-based state but also by those who have known all along the true purposes of revolutionary reorganization but managed for the time being to mask them skillfully.

I cannot agree that Mikhail Gorbachev, who has given up his make-believe optimism, wanted to see today's ugliness, ruin, and gloomy, outraged people. Nor did he look forward to having nothing to do but write his memoirs about the rebellious putschists. Even in purely personal terms, I am sure that it was never his secret wish to become a president without a state, a politician without a party, and a supreme commander-in-chief without an army. No leader in history, being of sound mind, has wanted to reach such a finale—a political suicide.

It is clear that our political express train has taken a sharp turn toward dictatorship. At the extraordinary Congress of People's Deputies of Russia, dominated by a weird mood of carefree expectations of doom, Boris Yeltsin received everything he wanted, including powers that no Russian autocrat possessed during the past three hundred years (even the Empress Anna Ivanovna's authority was limited).[18] Everything will depend on how and in whose interests he uses these powers. His first two "royal" decrees—the declaration of a state of emergency in Checheno-Ingushetia and the banning of his own CPSU, which had nurtured him—tell us a lot about the likely direction of his future moves.

Today, the wisest people in many countries are putting a great deal of thought into what to do with the former Soviet Union: to help it or not to help it? If it deserves some aid, how much and to whom and on what conditions? A curious proposal was suggested by Professor Alexander Yanov of the City University of New York.[19] His idea was that political modernization by our own people in our country is impossible. Russia, you see, has tried to do it already thirteen times since 1480—the year when it became a national state. He writes that without intellectual help, shared political experience, and economic support from the West, all reforms in our country are doomed to failure. The main task of the West is to tip the balance of forces inside Russia in favor of a real modernization, just like in the Russian fairy tale about a little mouse that adds its strength to the efforts of a whole team trying unsuccessfully to pull a turnip out of the ground, and, lo and behold, the turnip comes out!

However, while giving the West this magic power, our professor does not name the other members of the team who would do the pulling—in the fairy tale they are a grandfather, a grandmother, a granddaughter, and a dog. Does he believe that China, India, Brazil, and Mexico will join forces to help us out? This is highly unlikely: these countries have their own problems aplenty.

It is surprising that the intellectual portfolio of the democrats, whom the West has been assiduously helping all these years, appears to be totally empty. They have nothing to offer except vengeance, rancor, and speedy interdictions of this or that. It appears that the level of competence of the junior scholar–democrats is insufficient for the task. They do not know what to do. It is one thing to shout furiously "Down with them!" in Manezh Square and quite another to carry out success-fully reforms that affect the interests of millions of people.

I think that our Eurasian country can come out of the deepening crisis only by carrying out reforms of a Eurasian character based on the traditions, uniqueness, psychology, and interdependence of both continents—Asia and Europe. The central weakness of Gorbachev and Yeltsin as reformers has been their one-dimensional orientation and the absence of a systematic analysis of the transformations that they themselves started.

The remaining limited amount of public support makes it hardly possible to carry out radical reforms by democratic methods. But coer-cion is also doomed to failure, unless the population is first guaranteed a minimum standard of living, which evidently cannot be done. In essence, what we have is a stalemate.

Today, it is obvious to everyone that the existing problems can be solved only by first stabilizing the political situation, by preventing further chaos in the aftermath of the Soviet Union's collapse, and by extinguishing the fires of interethnic conflict that are engulfing much of Russia. Some people argue that it is already too late. The empire has collapsed, and what we see now are the natural consequences, which cannot be avoided. They evidently get some pleasure out of juggling new acronyms—USS [Union of Sovereign States], CIS [Common-wealth of Independent States], and so on—and are really anxious only about finding ways to prevent a possible spread of nuclear weapons and, of course, their use or misuse. At the same time, there is also talk about the inevitability of the collapse of all empires, illustrated by eloquent references to history. Unfortunately, such collapses were al-ways accompanied by bloody wars that went on until the shape of the new states that were built out of the fragments of the old empires emerged. This happened with Rome, the Ottoman Empire, and the vast expanses of Spain's holdings. Even in the comparatively small Austro-Hungarian Empire, centrifugal tendencies contributed to the outbreak of World War I, and the splitting up of this state into sovereign components created a major precondition leading to World War II.

But today we are talking about the disintegration of a huge "empire" encompassing one-sixth of the planet, armed with almost 30,000 nuclear warheads of tremendous destructive power, and with an abundance of worn-out nuclear reactors and deadly dangerous chemical plants.

Despite much talk of human rights, one aspect of this issue is overlooked: 75 million former Soviet citizens live outside their familiar national-territorial formations. There is virtually no family in our country that is not divided by the new sovereign borders and subjected to some degree of humiliation. Ethnic Russians find themselves in the worst situation. But as soon as people understand that they are the victims of an ambitious policy and a genocide unprecedented in peacetime, they will unite again, with or without weapons in their hands. And no agreement, signed in an office or a forest or among the bushes, will stop them. Two hundred years ago, Karamzin warned the Emperor Alexander I that all states were built upon conquests.[20] Today, some local [ethnic] leaders may hope that their home national guards could prevent new conquests of their "republics." Such hopes are an illusion. The creation of separate national guards in multinational states has always led to war among them. Such guards have not prevented violent conflicts in Yugoslavia, for example.

Although our situation clearly resembles that of Yugoslavia (on an infinitely larger scale), the possibility of a parallel development of events here has been minimized in our mass media. Our experienced politicians claim to rely fully on the loud assurances of the Kremlin leaders, although these leaders have not fulfilled earlier promises given to their own people. Only last summer, there was some talk of establishing international control over all former Soviet nuclear centers. Another rumored plan called for building a huge underground arms storage area in one location.

What took centuries to grow as a unified political body cannot be dismembered in an hour without bloody conflict. If the intoxication of sovereignty continues to prevail over common sense, the situation could get out of control. And a final tidal wave of the raging political-nationalistic storm could wash all of us away, including those who did their best to promote the disintegration of our country.

To keep this from happening, serious corrections should be made to the strategy of interstate relations, recognizing that Russia has exhausted its historical quota of revolutions and civil wars and that time for a nonapocalyptic disintegration of the "empire" is running out. If the idea of a new, unified, but interdependent commonwealth does not take root in our long-suffering land, no economic, financial, or humanitarian assistance from the West will be of any use to us. The same kind of chaos will emerge with which Russia has always responded to forced attempts to impose on it a lifestyle not suitable for its unique character.

We are entering the decisive stage of the formation of Russia's new state system. Once again, a narrow circle of close confidants is working out treaties, programs, and agreements affecting the destiny of every nation and the geopolitical balance of the entire world. As we know, the leadership of the Supreme Soviet of Russia has not even engaged in a preliminary discussion of the real effects of a shock-therapy transition to a market economy, not to mention measures of social protection, without which the trade unions would refuse to support such a program, as they have recently announced. In effect, a new kind of confrontation is being cultivated, this time not with the banned CPSU but with the largest organization of workers.

A state is not a rigid entity. It submits to the laws of development and changes its political shape and form accordingly. But whatever the sociopolitical system, there are certain basic elements without which a state cannot carry out its normal functions. These are a common economic space, a mechanism for tax and fiscal policy, uniform rights for the individual with the institutions to protect them, a language for interethnic intercourse, a system of basic social values, and a uniform defense and foreign policy. Without any one of these mainstays, the whole edifice of the state begins to collapse.

The current leadership [in the union republics] is already paying for its battle against the former political center of the USSR and its disregard for the laws governing every federative structure. After all, Russia is also a federated state, and any local leader joining the "parade of sovereignties" should be prepared for a similar display of stubbornness and selfishness on the part of any autonomous republic. But what would then be left for the Russian federative center? Where would the ongoing disintegration stop? This is a question not of political prestige but of the limits of sovereignty. Even more unseemly are the secret negotiations, conducted behind people's backs and contrary to their will as expressed in the recent [March 1991] referendum, to replace the Soviet Union with an amorphous confederation, semiconfederation, or commonwealth that would fall apart at the first vicissitude of fate. But as in everything else, our leaders are not guided by world experience. Are we really the only country that does not learn from its own errors or from the errors of others?

Our radical mass media, especially radio and television, seem unaware that Russia was the first but not the only great imperial state that at the beginning of this century stepped onto the road of revolutionary shock. After the Russian Empire began its radical political modernization in 1905, the Ottoman Empire followed suit in 1908, then China three years later, and then Japan and Germany in 1918. During the fifteen years of that era, some of the largest countries in the world were directly affected by powerful political explosions. True, some political scientists concluded that these states were unable to carry out overdue reforms because they lacked the decisive support of the traditional democracies. But just ten years later, the democracies themselves began to fall apart. By the autumn of 1929, even prosperous America suffered a most severe crisis, from which it recovered only by installing state regulatory mechanisms and programs of a truly socialist type.

The main reasons for those political shocks may have had little to do with a lack of talent among the monarchs and politicians and even less with the intrigues of the Bolsheviks. They had everything to do with the fact that the prevalence of private property and the egotistical psychology of the early twentieth century came into flagrant contradiction with public needs, compelling the ruling regimes to undertake a radical reorganization of economic relations. For most, it was much too little and far too late.

Our own experience during the following several decades demonstrated the polar extreme—that to rely completely on state property is just as bad and leads to the same impasse. Today's leaders have to find that golden middle ground—the optimum ratio between collective and personal interests—that can save the peoples of the planet from new suffering. Unfortunately, our modern Russian "revolutionaries" do not want to be involved in this laborious search. They prefer to take the line of least resistance and to follow the old path of designating new "enemies of the people."

Russia's history has witnessed many schisms. The religious split over three centuries ago resulted in many thousands of Old Believers leaving their villages and towns. The irreconcilable division between "proletarians" and "bourgeoisie" some seventy years ago swept away millions of lives. Today, as if the deep schisms dividing republics, generations, cities, and villages were not enough, the ruling regime wants to add another schism based on political beliefs and has already formulated a presidential decree that will make it the law of the land. Forty million of our ancestors, comrades and former and present members of the CPSU, are to be branded as criminals. But our Party did not consist only of scoundrels. Among its members were hundreds of thousands of people prominent in culture, science, and education. It was the party of Sholokhov, Zhukov, Korolyov, Chkalov—people honored by the whole world. We most certainly do not need another schism that would draw a dividing line through all our homes and families, pushing us, by intent or inadvertently, toward new confrontations, violence, and disorders.

For a long time in our political history we tried to fly using one wing alone, the left. Nothing good came of it, and now this wing is broken. The entire left half of the political space was left vacated, creating an extremely dangerous imbalance. Now this gap is being slowly filled by the nascent new parties. On the right, the "democrats" have taken power. They have shown some political inventiveness, remembering to borrow from overseas the term "mayors" and even "White House" and "Congress." But so far they have failed to borrow the most important thing—a stable two-party political system, the basic values of which are shared by all well-behaved Americans. But you will not get far on one wing; you will fly in circles, lose altitude, and then fall. If this happens, even those who have supported the "democrats" will realize that they have been deceived in their expectations.

Our one-wing country is really on the edge of an abyss, and the chaos in all aspects of life is growing worse. Political forces have been fragmented. Our leaders, who are endlessly dividing power and booty among themselves, have now reached the question of who should control the nuclear button. But who will unite us and how? For—I will repeat—no one will be saved separately. It must be all of us together. I see the new Russian All-People's Union movement as such a unifying force. It has simple and clear goals: justice, democracy, patriotism. I am sure that this movement could become the nucleus of a union of genuinely state-patriotic forces for whom to serve the people and the Fatherland will be the highest duty.

The Trial: Judges and Fates

In 1992, the Yeltsin regime tried unsuccessfully to have the Constitutional Court declare the entire former Communist Party of the Soviet Union a criminal organization (like the Nazi Party in Germany after World War II). Gennady Zyuganov was a key witness for its defense.

—V.M.

Honorable Court! I well understand that, in a country with "transparent" borders and a destroyed state administration, it is doubtful that a legal system can function normally. Nevertheless, as a person and a citizen, I sincerely wish the high court success in restoring constitutional legality and order in our tormented land.

Saltykov-Shchedrin once wrote: "The cruelty of Russia's laws has always been softened by the fact that they are not necessarily enforced." But today the failure to enforce laws has reached the point that it is causing general exasperation and lawlessness, which, unfortunately, affects this trial as well.

There is something unnatural and inhuman in the very fact that former members and leaders of the CPSU have essentially banned and are now trying to put on trial the party that gave birth to them. This means trampling on an eternal moral norm: children cannot judge their own parents. Another curious fact is that a nonparty attorney, Yu. Ivanov, is defending the CPSU, and a former member of the CPSU, A. Makarov, whose remarks at times remind us of Khazanov [a popular comedian], is its main prosecutor.

On the other hand, let us ponder the logic of the charges. The Party, whose ruling position was officially affirmed in the Constitution of the USSR, turns out to be unconstitutional. It is further alleged that the CPSU was not a party at all but a state, or a state structure, with its own constitution, the Charter of the CPSU. Moreover, the millions of persons who have passed through the Party, according to Makarov, are not on a par with ordinary citizens.

And all this is needed to justify, with masochistic lust, the destruction of the state and its constitutional foundations; to justify the chaos that reigns in our country and the violation of all international pacts on human rights; to camouflage the unprecedented betrayal of allies and friends, relatives, the elderly, and children. It is needed to justify the appropriation of property acquired by the labor of three generations of Soviet people. And this outrage is occurring not on a commodity exchange or in a marketplace but in the Constitutional Court—our last hope for a legal outcome to a lengthy litigation.

Honorable Court! In my view this is such a perversion of justice, logic, and conscience that it cannot be commented on within the framework of common sense. The logic of the charges should not be the object of inquiry of this Constitutional Court but rather of some other institution. I realize that an irrational consciousness is dominant in our society, thanks to the type of relations being introduced in which one person steals from nine others and promises to share the booty with them later. Of course, everybody knows that such relations can be based only on big lies and much violence, with the rights of the individual completely suppressed and laws disregarded. And even then, this can last only a short time.

Nevertheless, despite the conditions reigning here in the Constitutional Court, I would like to focus in my statement on two issues: the so-called "state of the CPSU" and the impact of this trial on the deepening schism of our society. The choice of these issues is not dictated by my desire but rather by the character of the charges, which are purely formal and disassociated from the pain and fate of millions today, when all that happened in the past is impudently presented as the result of the intrigues of the illegal CPSU.

According to this hind-sight logic, members of this "illegal organization" included all the front-line commanders during the Great Patriotic War, from Georgy Zhukov to Nikolai Vatutin; all the main designers and directors of factories, from Sergei Korolyov to Yevgeny Paton; half of our writers and professors; and, if you will excuse me, a majority of the people present in this courtroom.[21]

Think about it: some 40 million people have passed through the CPSU in all its years of existence. And since the average size of a family in our country consists of four or five people, this means that a minimum of 160 million of our citizens were in one way or another connected with this illegal—and some allege criminal—organization. And those who accuse us today were yesterday not only members of the CPSU but leaders issuing commanding instructions. I believe that even such villains as Vyshinsky, Beria, and Yagoda could not see anything like this in their worst nightmares.[22]

It is well known that every political and legal system has its own capacities. In our instance, the need for reforms had been obvious to everyone. That is why the absolute majority of our citizens actively supported the transformations started by the Party in the middle of the 1980s and, above all, the creation of a full-fledged Republic of Soviets, relieving the Party of the unusual functions it had been compelled to assume, especially in the years of the Great Patriotic War. Our esteemed professors of history have convincingly spoken about this, but, unfortunately, their statements have been hushed up by the so-called independent and free democratic press.

But the reform process did not reach the country at large, and soon it was led astray in anticonstitutional and antistate ways. Let me remind you that in the mid-1960s a whole special program was developed, and it was not called perestroika or radical reform. It was a program aimed at undermining the country's constitutional structure and at destroying the USSR as a uniform and great power. Its key item and basic component was the statement that it would be impossible to blow apart the USSR from within without first destroying the CPSU. But the CPSU could only be destroyed from the top, by penetrating the decision-making centers of the Party and the state. This could not be accomplished from the bottom up.

Honorable Court, please give your attention to the basic conceptual ideas formulated in the various documents pertaining to this program. Many of them are no longer secret. They can be summarized in five points:

• first—to portray the USSR as the last and most predatory empire on earth and to undertake everything possible to destroy it;

• second—to prove that the USSR was not the chief architect of victory in the Great Patriotic War but was as villainous as fascism, that this country does not deserve any respect;

• third—to escalate the arms race and deform completely the Soviet economy, which was already undermined by the war; to prevent the USSR from carrying out social programs that could demonstrate the true essence of the state system and its attractiveness;

• fourth—to fire up nationalism, and with support from national-religious extremism, to blow the country apart from within;

• fifth—to seize control of the mass media with the help of "influence agents" and try to destroy the collective foundations of people's lives in our state by once again cutting our people's present off from the past and depriving them of the future.

Consciously or not, this program was put into high gear after Gorbachev, Yakovlev, and Shevardnadze assumed power. If you read closely the articles in the newspaper *Moscow News* and in the magazine *Ogonyok* of that period, you can easily notice signs pointing out ways to realize this program.[23] They were in effect orders, which were then multiplied and distributed across the entire country to form a destructive, antinational policy.

The most effective successor of this line under present conditions is the newspaper *Izvestia*. It is no accident that this newspaper has become the focal point for heated debates in the Supreme Soviet of Russia. This is not glasnost, as we are being assured by the journalist Yevgeny Kiselev on his program "Itogi," but a free hand to continue manipulating public opinion with completely alien positions and values.

I have personally prepared many reports on conditions in Lithuania and the Caucasus, about the work of their soviets and law-enforcement institutions—all of which were shelved by the leadership. Under the guise of creating a civil society, a law-based state, democracy, pluralism, sovereignty, and independence, the constitutional foundations of the state—the Congress and the Supreme Soviet of the USSR, the people's oversight—were all destroyed, and the army and the law-and-order establishment were all but destroyed as well. The tool of this destructive policy was a fundamentally new weapon, which has yet to be studied very thoroughly—informational-psychological programming using huge capacities, which has succeeded in causing dissent and discord within our society and has proven to be more powerful than the fascist hordes in World War II.

However, the basic causes of our tragedy were inside our own state, foremost in the monopolized economy and the moral-political character of its leadership.

Honorable Court! I cannot assert, as some others do, that the Party is not guilty of anything. This would be far from the truth. The Party is above all guilty of having exercised exclusive power for a long time, as a result losing its sense of political struggle, its ability to analyze conditions accurately, and the support of the masses. In the process of democratization, the CPSU was obligated to begin with itself by bringing into leadership positions talented, state-oriented people with a real love for Russia instead of people who call Russia "this country." Such new people would have been able to find an evolutionary way to carry out urgently needed reforms. They would have understood that complex state systems can be modernized only one part at a time. Otherwise, you end up with a loss of control and complete chaos of the kind that we are witnessing everywhere today.

The Central Committee of the CPSU unfortunately did not have enough courage to relieve Gorbachev of his duties even when his complete inability to lead the Party and the state, his moral unscrupulousness, and his violation of his public oath became obvious. Amazingly, this winner of the Nobel Peace Prize, who unleashed a civil war in his own country, lowered the state flag from the Kremlin, and appropriated a whole city block of CPSU property, is continuing to give advice on how we should live and work.

Many of us did not have enough political sense and courage to object when President Yeltsin, traveling all over the country and promising everyone boundless sovereignty, committed himself to the creation of an independent state with just three functions: unified defense, transport, and energy systems (now the last of these is not even included). The idea was not only unconstitutional but also politically illiterate. Every professional person knows that a state rests on seven pillars, at a minimum, and is in danger of collapse if any one of them falters. These pillars are a uniform economic and territorial space, a uniform system of finances and taxes, a uniform language of interethnic exchange, uniform human rights protected by the state, and uniform defense and foreign policies.

We did not react appropriately to an extremely disturbing signal, when in respectable Estonia they started talking seriously about the priority of one nationality above another and initiating clashes among nationalities within the entire country. Now, in independent Estonia, brown passports for so-called Russian-speaking persons are being issued. Even the racists in South Africa did not allow themselves to do such a thing. Latvia went even further: for several months they have been finding out who in the leadership has a Russian wife. Such a marriage is judged to be a compromising circumstance.

Genuine citizens of our Fatherland worried about its integrity and destiny have been fed one after another to voracious journalists acting on the orders of Alexander Yakovlev, that master of undercover intrigues. Just remember the case of General Rodionov, who [in April 1989] was the only member of the Georgian Politburo to vote against the use of troops to disperse demonstrators in Tbilisi.[24] For that he was immediately removed from his post as military district commander.

Later a large number of our compatriots were added to this blacklist, and some of them are actually still behind the walls of Matrosskaya Tishina Prison. And look at the barrage of accusations hurled at the courageous Russian general Alexander Lebed, who has honestly informed us about the ongoing genocide [against Moldova's Russian minority] in the Dniester Region![25]

Most of all, the Party is guilty of allowing incompetent opportunists to come to power, people who did not understand the constitutional foundations of our state and the specific features of Russia and the Soviet Union as a unique national-state entity. They are the people who have also ignored the historical and political experience of all other countries. This experience teaches that the constitutions of all countries proceed from the premise that the first priority is to protect territorial security. It is easy to see why: all states were founded on conquests, and hardly any state has been destroyed without bloody wars. As we can see, we are no exception. In the wake of the destruction of the USSR, war fires are burning ever hotter in Central Asia, the Caucasus, and the Dniester Region.

Summarizing what has been presented above, I can state that the issue is not the constitutionality of the CPSU. Its constitutionality has nothing to do with the charges. All the efforts of Mr. Makarov to present here one more "confession on the given theme,"[26] in my view, have been in vain. The same goes for his attempts to impress the High Court with such emotional expressions as "proletarian petty bureaucrats," "party bonzes," or "trembling hands and cheeks," which simply underscore the legal weakness of his speech. As for the RCP [Russian Communist Party], there was not a single argument in his speech supporting the allegation that it violated the laws of Russia in the past, aside from the fact that it was a part of the CPSU! But if you follow the reasoning of Mr. Makarov far enough, you will see that it makes no sense. The CPSU was a party of the USSR, which, according to the "democrats," no longer exists. (However, I believe that the Soviet Union does exist and will certainly be restored.) But if we are talking here about a party of another state, this Honorable Constitutional Court is apparently exceeding its own authority and invading the prerogatives of the CIS, which still has no similarly lofty judicial body of its own.

As for the Russian Communist Party, I want to mention that, after Russia's declaration of sovereignty, according to which Russia's laws were to have precedence over those of the Soviet Union (which was one of the main reasons for the collapse of the Soviet Union), the Russian Communist Party cannot even be considered as being legally a part of the CPSU because its sovereignty is above that of the CPSU. It is therefore likely that this High Court will have no choice but to permit it to resume normal work in the near future.

Honorable Court! Why has Deputy Oleg Rumyantsev, by bringing in the second question, drawn us into this fruitless, extremely dangerous litigation? Is it not clear that the country is like dry wood soaked with gasoline? Look around you: banditry and racketeering are on the rampage, rivers of weapons flow from the South and the West to the Center, peasants refuse to deliver grain to the state (remember 1928 and what followed), all large-scale production is about to come to a halt, and soon Manezh Square in Moscow will be filled not with vendors but with those who feed themselves by their own labor. I believe that all this was done deliberately, not accidentally. Although I am of the opinion that the "democrats" made an inexcusable error in banning the activity of the CPSU, it has not been a unified entity for a long time. At its next Congress, it would have divided into two wings, giving our country three large political centers capable of engaging in a constructive debate. In this way, true democracy could have come into existence, although its development, naturally, would have been difficult. But this way everything has been turned into a political mess, which is conducive to the rise of a dictatorship, although the essential prerequisites are lacking even for a dictatorship: a strong army, the support of a significant part of the population, and a smoothly working system of law-enforcement agencies.

There are, however, many candidates for the role of dictator—the leader of the "democratic" movement, Gavriil Popov, for example. In an article published in the French paper *Libération*, he brazenly called for the seizure of power by a "thin upper layer," which could suppress the "majority of Russians" and force the country to proceed to a free market—of the mafia type, no doubt. As you can see, Popov is quite ready. He had a stint as mayor of Moscow and managed to transform the city into a world garbage dump; now he wants to sit on the Russian throne—provided, as he wrote, that he is "not obligated to undergo examinations by election" and not "subject to people's sanctions." What a rare democrat he is!

And yet, I believe that our opponents are trying to solve three major strategic problems with this trial.

First, by artificially associating the state with the Party, they want to finalize the collapse of the Soviet Union and vindicate their disregard of the people's will expressed in the national referendum. They want to do it here, in the Constitutional Court, a high and respected institution, thereby putting it in an ambiguous situation as the supreme guardian of justice.

Second, they want to avoid personal responsibility for the failure of their radical reforms by putting the blame on the former communists and on the national-patriotic state forces, who understand perfectly that the sovereign republics cannot survive alone in our country, for an entity that has endured for centuries cannot be divided in one hour by anyone.

Third, they want to be able, as a last resort, to use this legal decision to prosecute and rout all inconvenient people—whether directors of factories, or officers of the Soviet Army or state security, or obstinate writers and our own businessmen—under the pretext that the absolute majority of them were members of the CPSU and could thus be declared "criminals."

The ultimate goal of this strategy is to bring to completion the destruction of a united Russia capable of asserting national and state interests and carrying out independent policies. The last meeting of the "G–7" in Munich confirmed the goals of this strategy. Our huge oil fields were offered to Germany for exploitation in payment for our debts, and the United States unambiguously demanded the transfer of the Southern Kuriles to Japan, tying this condition to promised economic aid, which no one has yet seen.

Our country has been artificially pushed toward a new schism based on ideological-national attributes: if you think differently, you are an opponent; if you are of a different nationality, you are an enemy. This schism could be even more terrible than in 1917, when over 650,000 members of the national-state elite, whose profession was to serve the Fatherland, were summarily outlawed. The purged group included high-ranking imperial officials, gentry, officers, businessmen, professors, clergy, Cossacks, and others. Our grandfathers and fathers made peace among themselves only after the bloodbath of the mass repressions and the Great Patriotic War.

This time, we had every opportunity to carry out the appropriate reforms slowly, without extremist radicalism. But this is not what happened. To this day, our new revolutionaries cannot control their itch to settle accounts. The current Soviet elite was almost all part of the CPSU. Although the CPSU contained many scoundrels, turncoats, and traitors, to find the entire Party illegal would amount to a mass condemnation of the Russian national elite, which would be absolutely ruinous for our state and especially its intellectual-administrative sphere. This would be a great tragedy for Russia. It could be the end of Russia. I, however, continue to believe that no one would succeed in doing this one more time to our country.

Honorable Court! We are entitled to expect a fair decision in the matter before you. At the same time, regardless of your pending verdict, I want to inform you that the united opposition, the bloc of national-patriotic forces, and the Russian National Assembly will do everything to prevent a new fratricide, a recurrence of 1937, and the emergence of a new compradorian *oprichnina* [secret police] in our Fatherland. Should it become necessary, we will turn directly to the nation's public opinion and find the courage to stop provocateurs of a new confrontation in Russia and to nail the political adventurers to the pillar of shame forever.

With its 1.5 million refugees, thousands of nuclear warheads, and an abundance of worn-out nuclear reactors and dangerous chemical plants, Russia has exhausted its capacity for revolutions and civil wars. It is left with two remaining ways to settle disputes and controversies: dialogue and law. We are ready for this, and we hope that the High Court is interested in seeing that these two remedies become the main instruments for settling the disputes of politicians and the final argument of today's kings.

Let me make a brief remark in conclusion. When I was listening to the many-hour-long speech of the attorney Makarov, which sounded more like a public prosecutor's verdict, I constantly found myself thinking that all this had a familiar ring, that I had read it somewhere before. Now I know why. I recommend to Mr. Makarov, who now has access to the Party archives, that he look up the materials of the Sixteenth Party Congress of 1930 and closely read the text of a statement given there by Comrade Kirshon, who thundered against Russian national literature, culture, and philosophy, condemned the great scholar Alexei Losev for every imaginable sin, and recommended that for holding the wrong philosophical views Losev should be place before a firing squad.[27] Fortunately, Losev was not executed, but he was imprisoned for a long time. He was eventually released and lived to be more than ninety years old, departing our world as a philosopher of world renown. Kirshon's own destiny was more tragic: he was executed before a firing squad in 1938.

The point I am trying to make is that all of us, including the attorneys who have become involved in higher politics, are obligated to learn the necessary lessons from history and to calculate our moves at least two or three steps ahead. This applies also to Mr. Makarov.

We Will Withstand and Win

Russia is experiencing a truly unique period in its history. A historical rollback is taking place disguised as "democracy" and "a return to the world community." In practice, a political shift is occurring behind the scenes that fits the concept of a counterrevolution. It began approximately in 1989, reached its peak in August 1991, and at the moment is metastasizing throughout all the strata of our society and all the spheres of the economy, in the process changing the fundamental principles of human relations.

But it would be a political error to limit this shift, this counterrevolution, to any timeframe. The initial stage of the actual systemic crisis dates back to the 1970s, when socialism in the USSR gradually began to lose its historical initiative. At that time, the CPSU could no longer adequately address new problems in the domestic and international spheres, and its top echelon showed signs of moral, political, and ideological degradation.

Parallel with these crisis phenomena, shadow capital was developing and shadow economic, financial, and subpolitical structures were being created. Gradually, these structures penetrated the state apparatus, its economic complex, and its political system, including the CPSU network, all the way up to the highest levels of power.

By the middle of the 1980s, the country's leaders and the people at large began to realize that they needed to find a way out of the crisis situation, improve their economy, and democratize life in general. By this time, the shadow economy was running out of space for expanded reproduction; consequently, its bosses raised the question of how to weaken political restraints by influencing the state and Party apparatus, including the CPSU Central Committee, from the inside. It was under such pressures that perestroika came into existence. From the start, it was a political double deal. Its leaders, from Gorbachev, Yakovlev, and Shevardnadze to Gorbunovs [of Latvia] and Snegur [of Moldova], used propaganda to disorient people. Behind this smokescreen, they nourished the idea of a radical change of the political system, culminating in the open counterrevolution of August 1991.

The statement regarding the uniqueness of the present historical period is not accidental. The political movement backward is phenomenal by itself. Perhaps the most amazing fact is that wild capitalism is being imposed on Russia under conditions in which political authority is already changing and adapting the superstructure of society while the economic system and the formal management complex still retain a public (state) character. Shadow capital and its owners, the political-economic mafia, have gained a political victory and taken power, but they have not advanced a single step in the economic sphere. In this sense, the current political power in Russia is baseless, and, at the same time, the state (public) economic organism and the social strata of the population related to it are outside politics. Realizing this, it is easy to understand why the Yeltsin regime is striving to take over the national property, which can only be done through the dictatorship of a small group of legalized shadow businessmen and their political lobbyists. Hence the feverish movements aimed at creating a so-called presidential republic. It is also easy to predict the growth of political activity in all strata of society, which have lost their basic rights, including the right to work, against this further alienation of public (state) property.

Collisions of economic interests cause political confrontations—even bloodshed. This is the bottom line of all revolutions, as well as counterrevolutions. However speedy and triumphant a political revolution, its ultimate success or defeat is determined by the outcome of the struggle of political-economic interests, a struggle that is accelerated by the momentum of the revolution or counterrevolution. The 1917 October Revolution was followed by a civil war, which we now perceive as a national tragedy. Since August 1991 and the subsequent actions of the Yeltsin political regime, a new national tragedy is looming on our horizon. Complete responsibility for such a tragedy will be borne by the regime, which has neither understood nor learned anything from the scholarship of Marxism-Leninism or from the Chicago school of economic enslavement. This regime, realizing the limiting narrowness of its social base, has started to generate compradorian bourgeois supporters, who are closely connected with transnational corporations and Western mafia structures and who pump the riches of Russia and their capital to the West. This is what makes the current regime antinational and a paid agent of transnational political centers outside our country.

The union of the political regime, legalized shadow capital, and foreign political-economic structures leaves no room for our own national entrepreneurship, which is consequently aspiring to be involved in the sphere of the opposition's activity and at this stage is an ally of the humiliated and plundered working people.

For all practical purposes, we can now offer a picture of the distribution of political forces in Russia. On the one hand, a political regime leaning on a corrupt state apparatus and a mafia-compradorian bourgeoisie. Even by creating its own vertical chain of command (representatives of the president, administrative heads, executive structures), this regime has neither the ability nor the possibility to control conditions in the country or steer political-economic processes. That is why its aim is to switch to a regime of personal authority, that is, to create a dictatorship. The provocative actions of Yeltsin on December 10, 1992, the unfair manipulations of the referendum on the draft Constitution,[28] and the creation of a new antinational "democratic bloc" are all steps leading to a dictatorship that would permit the use of any method, including repression, to strengthen the political regime and bolster the power of compradorian and supranational capital.

On the other side are all the plundered people—workers, peasants, working intelligentsia, scientists, cultural workers, and military personnel. Dozens of political parties, movements, and public organizations, including professional associations, are vying for political representation. The deprived people are represented in the legislative body by this joint opposition, which has little or no influence on executive authority and is insufficiently organized. This poorly put-together "multivoiced mass" testifies to the current weakness of our political organizations, but, simultaneously, it nurtures a broad political movement capable of preventing a national-state catastrophe and initiating a righteous cause to revive the country.

All valid opposition movements and parties are characterized by a strongly expressed aspiration to defend the state's integrity, support national revival, and ensure political stability. The program documents of these parties—from monarchists and nationalists to communists and socialists—assert these principles. And all are in opposition to the present political regime. A significant number of parties of various ideological and political coloring have declared themselves ready to defend the interests of labor, the classes, and social groups. By doing so, they have deprived the communists and socialists of a monopoly on the interests of workers, peasants, and the working intelligentsia. Certainly, it is possible to claim that these are mere verbal declarations, but now the communists and socialists will have to show by concrete deeds that they are firmly tied to the working and exploited people. Neither historical memoirs nor the purity of their Marxism-Leninism can help. Only real, concrete work will now be accepted as proof of the truthfulness of their political manifestos and theoretical-ideological positions. To avoid falling into sectarianism and dogmatism, we must clearly recognize this fact as we prepare for the restoration congress of the Communists of Russia.

At the same time, the declared expression of national-state interests gives us a basis for the creation of a broad coalition opposing the antinational and antistate regime. All opposition parties and movements recognize that a catastrophe has engulfed Russia and that this catastrophe can be overcome only through the cooperation of left and right, believers and atheists, working people and nationally oriented businessmen. Such national unity already existed before, in the years of the Great Patriotic War, when a significant part of the white emigration participated in the Resistance and helped the Red Army, Soviet Russia, and the USSR any way it could. At that time the communist Mikhail Sholokhov and the anticommunist Ivan Bunin both unequivocally believed in our eventual victory.[29] All were united by their devotion to Mother Russia and their hatred of the occupiers. To ignore this lesson would be inexcusable. Now again it is much more important to save Russia than to preserve one's ideological innocence. To be more exact, now, in the face of a national-state tragedy, ideological and political disagreements become secondary. The fundamental problem now is to strengthen the unity of the opposition forces for the sake of Russia's salvation.

Only such a united bloc can bring to power a government of national salvation, and only such a united opposition can save the country and its people from the tragedy of a new civil war, after which there would be no victors and no losers left in Russia, and the Russian state itself would most likely not survive. In spite of the screams of the treacherous "democratic mass media," we, the opposition, have every right to call ourselves the party of peace and national consensus. This should be reflected in the program documents of the Communist Party and in its actions.

The fact that the events of recent years were manifestations of a national-state catastrophe instigated to a large extent from abroad and that each additional day of the Yeltsin political regime prolongs the loss of our state independence and sovereignty leads to one more important conclusion. The reborn Communist Party of Russia should make patriotism its banner in the struggle for the minds and hearts of our people, while remaining faithful to the historical achievement of friendship among all peoples living in Russia. In this way, we will strengthen our people's confidence in the party of workers, allow the communists to find reliable allies, and help establish a constructive dialogue and cooperation in the whole spectrum of opposition parties and movements. In doing this, given the efforts to impose on human-kind a barracks lifestyle in the "new world order," our struggle for the revival of Russia will become a contribution to the fulfillment of our international duty. Only a powerful Russia will be able to prevent the coming of a one-dimensional existence under the conditions of a new world order and allow all peoples to live according to their historical traditions, spiritual values, and long-developed ideals. Fostering Russia's return to great-power status is now a natural goal of the opposition in general and of the reborn Communist Party in particular.

By resisting the perestroika catastrophe and struggling against "democratic genocide," we have proved our loyalty to the working people and the entire nation. We have also proved that the Communists can meet the challenge of nihilism and antinational obscurantism. We see a future Russia in all its greatness, power, and prosperity enjoying complete spiritual and ideological diversity. Russia will restore the brotherhood of nations that was crushed by the so-called "universal human values" in the center and by the nationalistic demagogues at the local level. History is not over—Russia is alive, is struggling, and will win.

At a Sharp Bend in the Road

Any radical transition of a society is complicated, painful, and bound to result in hardships. Anyone who does not understand this or does not want to accept the inevitable costs of progress is a defender of the old system. This is the argument that my most diligent opponents use to justify their disagreement with my recent articles.

This is the one and only argument amidst a flood of curses and threats pouring down on me from the pages of many publications. But this gives me the opportunity to continue the dialogue without the rancor that has recently become characteristic of our "pluralism of opinions."

So progress is inconsistent and one has to pay for everything. This is absolutely correct for all times and peoples. But by virtue of its abstraction, its application to the present situation requires a particularly careful analysis, which is being evaded by my opponents. Even the historian A. Kiva, who remembered everything from Vologda butter to smoked ham, has not yet delved into a historical interpretation of the period of perestroika. Supporters of "progress" should know that the price paid for it is not unimportant, because it is possible to pay so dearly that you end up bankrupt. Indeed, such cases have not been a rarity.

Any change comprises in itself an element of preservation, otherwise it is not a change but rather a disintegration. In spite of all the discussions about the inevitability of destroying the old order, the culture and humanism that comprise its core should, nevertheless, be retained and nurtured. A genuine revolution is different from a "senseless and ruthless" rebellion, because social changes, however drastic, are made with continuity and with care for the improvement of the basic conditions of human development.

But our society is losing its feeling of self-preservation. The situation is so desperate that the question is not about what "-ism" to build next in our country but about physical and spiritual survival—to be or not to be?

The heirs of the Komsomol who speak about "overcoming alienation" and "increasing degrees of freedom" have in some places already stepped over the red line.[30] In video salons, pornography, horror, and violence are shown to young children and teenagers. The timid protests of indignant parents drown in this murky stream of indecency. Excited by what they see on the videos, boys go into the streets and repeat the "lessons" they learned. I think that not everyone realizes that the doubling of the teenage crime rate in many regions over just two years will soon bring a sharp increase in the number of repeat criminals. If the moral foundation of a person is destroyed at a young age, it is extremely difficult to restore. While we are hypnotizing ourselves with discussions about "humanization and discovery of the true self," time-delayed mines are being placed under society. History tells us that the most reliable way to get rid of aboriginal peoples is to turn them into drunkards. As you can see, we are being made into "addicts" by much more potent means.

Predatory market forces are stealthily encroaching on the fundamental sciences and breaking apart and destroying the scientific-technological potential of our country—our last remaining hope for a dignified way out of the crisis. We created the rocket *Buran*, a miracle of engineering. This allowed us to create 500 new unique technologies—an entirely new industrial culture! Today its creators have been laid off and have to work for cooperatives making knickknacks—the state has no funds.

If this is the price we must pay for the next phantom of a "glorious future," I am categorically against such "progress." But I am sure progress has nothing to do with it. All civilized states know that the market is not an end in itself but a means that requires constant regulation. They recognize that politics is fruitless if it is not based on economics. In culture, education, science, defense, crime, and social justice, no one counts on sponsors and charity. The state, responsible to its citizens, must take these spheres under its supervision, control, and management. It is the task of the state to ensure the viability and sustainability of society and to create those frameworks and conditions without which freedom degenerates into chaos and barbarism.

But instead of strengthening these frameworks, already weakened in the "epoch of stagnation," our politicians continue their destruction. This shows a lack of responsibility, a misunderstanding of the essence of statehood, a direct undermining of market relations, and the absence of a strong state policy in the social sphere. Even in the now criticized 1960s, the share of funds channeled from national revenues into the development of science and education was twice as high as it is today.

Some politicians pretend to be amazed by the interethnic conflicts in our country. But many people living in these republics have already long been living by different laws. It is obvious that even the most correct teams playing in the same game but following different rules will inevitably fight. This is what inequality and discrimination in ethnic relations brings.

A state is certainly not an inflexible entity frozen in time. It obeys the logic of development and changes its political shape accordingly.

However, blinded by perestroika enthusiasm and angry nihilism, the ultrarevolutionaries are recklessly destroying the building of our statehood, which they have condemned and labeled totalitarian.

Let us assume that the state does collapse. What would follow—a radioactive meltdown? We can already feel its hot breath.

I think there is another road to the future. It leads through strengthening and developing the federal state that had historically formed in our country, clearly differentiating between the rights and duties of the center and those of the sovereign republics. As an indispensable condition for renewing our Union, we must sign new and binding Union and Federal agreements.

But there are many public figures who do not see and do not want to see any of this. At the very moment when the Americans renounced the label "evil empire," this label was picked up inside our country and promoted to the rank of a political doctrine. Now the image of the "last colonial empire" is being vigorously implanted into the public consciousness. This may be a good time to recollect the experience of the United States, where even verbal calls for the disintegration of the country are severely punishable under the law.

But in Russia the process of feudal disintegration is being persistently encouraged. Gavriil Popov has not merely proposed the formation of fifty nuclear ministates with disputable borders "out of the fragments of the empire" but, with the energy peculiar to him, is working on the creation of a new Moscow "principality." A similar recommendation was made by Hitler's chief intellectual adviser, Dr. Abel, who developed the Eastern Plan to enslave and destroy the USSR. This expanding epidemic of total "sovereignization" has nothing in common with the splendid idea of the interdependence of the world. It is nothing more than the naive notion, doomed to failure, that salvation can be achieved separately, which in reality only exacerbates the general chaos and devastation. Its logical end calls for absolutely "independent" individuals, each sitting in his or her own cellar armed with a sawed-off shotgun.

Only vigorous and energetic businessmen with initiative can rescue Russia today! This appeal is sounding louder and louder from the camp of the "democrats," and under its banner a new mass political party is being organized. Its publicists portray a decent society in which the "enrichment of one benefits all." But they do not mention that there are two kinds of business—civilized and criminal-speculative. The lat-

ter lurches in a destructive direction, gravitating to financial speculation, racketeering, drugs, and prostitution. A black marketeer never
voluntarily becomes a farmer. He would rather arm himself to assert
his "legal rights" than change his occupation. Harsh laws are being
used all over the world in the battle against such criminal-speculative
businessmen. Look, for example, at what is going on to fight organized
crime in Colombia.

The capital in our country—nine-tenths of which has a criminal
origin—stems from the era before anyone ever heard of perestroika,
when the union of a shadow economy, organized crime, and a corrupt
bureaucracy was already prospering in the blatant and refined plunder
of working people. The transfer of power into the hands of this union
(and our country is just a few steps away from this) will be the con-
cluding chord in a long ongoing process. And this will spell the end of
our great multinational state. Our domestic mafia, stealing its way to
power, has sufficiently revealed its basic antipublic, antistate, and antinational character.

I doubt that any additional evidence is needed after exposures in the
press of the slimy acts committed by the "democratic" authorities.
Doctor of Economic Sciences Tatyana Koryagina, a people's deputy of
the RSFSR, honestly and convincingly told us about some of them. In
one single affair, which was fortunately stopped in time despite vigorous attempts to whitewash it, a 140 billion ruble sale to international
criminals would have resulted in an avalanche of spontaneous
privatization and the loss of national sovereignty over almost half the
material wealth of Russia.

But who can guarantee that other similar deals are not being made
or contemplated today? The whole monitoring system of the state has
been destroyed. Without its restoration and strict observance of the
laws, it will not be possible to carry out any reform. The same is true
of the entire infrastructure.

I am sure that the nouveaux riches cannot long retain state power in
their hands or protect the national interests of the peoples of the Soviet
Union and the Russian Federation. All they are capable of is plundering, selling the national wealth, and destroying the country's integrity.

The present unfolding of events is in some respects reminiscent of
the summer of 1917, depicted by General Denikin in his *Essays on the
Russian Time of Troubles*. "Something unimaginable is happening in
our country! . . . Anarchy. Disorders. Pogroms. Mob law . . . Banditry

and robberies on all railroads and on all waterways! ... The most fertile regions are perishing! Soon nothing will be left but the naked ground!"[31] These were the fruits of the worthless rule of an outworn czarist regime and the eight-month-long attempt of the Provisional Government to correct the situation. They proved their inability to rule over Russia.

Today, in newspapers and magazines with circulations in the millions and in thousands of hours of radio and television broadcasts, cynical lies are being told about the "irresponsible Bolshevik experiment" in Russia in 1917, which is alleged to be the source of today's problems. An honest historian will tell a different story.

On the eve of the October Revolution, Lenin wrote an anticrisis program entitled "The Threatening Catastrophe and How to Fight It." What was it about? It was about disorder in transportation and industry, unemployment, and approaching famine. And about the fact that the measures to fight this catastrophe were well known, not invented by the Bolsheviks, and had been tested in practically all countries engaged in the war. He pointed out that the ruling classes of Russia appeared unable to implement these measures.

Only the working people and the Soviet government could rescue Russia and assert its national interests. Nikolai Berdyaev, who had no sympathy for the Soviet regime, recognized the "indisputable merit of communism to the Russian state."[32] Recall his testimony: "Russia was under the threat of complete anarchy and disintegration. This was stopped by the communist dictatorship, which found slogans the people were willing to obey."

What took place later is another matter—important, but nevertheless different. I am convinced that the subsequent tragic events were connected not with socialist ideas but with a deviation from these ideas, not with revolution but with quiet, creeping counterrevolution. The transformation of this counterrevolution into a very loud one made the situation even more tragic. This is why I would treasure the goals of genuine perestroika: a humane renewal of society, a return of power to the soviets, that is, to the people; and the creation of genuine democracy and a truly law-based state. Any other way leads nowhere.

But to move along the path of renewal, it is necessary to engage in the most essential, urgent business. Our most important goals should be the preservation of the country and its unique multinational and cultural-historical values and the preservation of its economic and po-

litical integrity. I believe that an overwhelming majority of my countrymen will join me in this cause.

A time of troubles never comes without false prophets, vaudeville
stage politicians, political narcissists, costly advisers who can guess in
advance the ideas and actions of their bosses, not to mention the indispensable "ideological" yes-men, who appear in too large numbers even
during normal times.

However, when you see how the writer Valentin Rasputin is honestly asserting the honor and conscience of the nation, how confidently
and professionally Sergei Baburin is struggling against the encroach-
ment of the clan regime, how General Boris Gromov is courageously
protecting our true statehood, and how the scholar Ramazan Abdulatipov is cleverly and consistently defending the friendship of nations,
you cannot but feel confident that reason and common sense will prevail.[33]

These are all, of course, very different people. But they are united
by their belief that a genuine basis for consent and consolidation is that
civic spirit which we have inherited from the best sons and daughters
of Russia and without which the most eloquent talk about humanism
and friendship will degenerate into a great lie and new tyrants.

Eurasia—Fate and Challenge

Today, many citizens of the USSR comprehend the catastrophic consequences of the destruction of their huge country. Most of us are rising
through the tragedy to a new level of spirituality and thought. To us,
the efforts of those who tried to understand the disintegration and then
restoration of the Russian Empire after 1917 are priceless today. We
include in this legacy the powerful voice of the "Eurasians"—proponents of a scholarly and political movement that arose during the 1920s.

In 1921, four emigrés from Russia—Pavel Savitsky, Pyotr Suvchin-
sky, Nikolai Trubetskoy, and Georges Florovsky—published the book
*Exodus to the East: Presentiments and Accomplishments. Affirmation
of the Eurasians*.[34] This intellectual and ideological movement quickly
received wide recognition among Russian emigrants in Europe, drawing hostility from right-wing circles and an enthusiastic response from
young people.

From its beginning, Eurasianism was the creative response of the

Russian national consciousness to the Russian Revolution and the ensuing civil war. The philosopher Berdyaev, in this connection, created the aphorism: "Eurasianism is the dread of and a reaction against revolutions." But this was not a dread that leads away from reality; this was the reaction of thinkers who took a new look at Russia from a perspective that combined their deep knowledge of geography, history, ethnology, and linguistics.

In 1927, the Committee of Eurasians in the USSR formulated a credo:[35]

> Who are the Eurasians? What do they want to achieve? Eurasians are those who have revealed Russia as a special cultural-historical world. They are those for whom Russia is not just a state but one-sixth of the world; not Europe and not Asia but a special middle continent—Eurasia with its self-assertive culture and a special historical fate. To copy Western forms of life is unnatural for Russia-Eurasia. Such copying has entailed and will continue to entail the hardest shocks for our country. Russia has no need for either a police autocracy of the Prussian type or a parliamentary democracy that camouflages the dictatorship of European and world capital. As for communism, which proclaimed a battle against capitalism but, having been itself generated by European capitalism, has deceived the expectations of the working people—it has degenerated into a form of rule by a corrupt bureaucracy.

Proceeding from their acceptance of the specific features of Russian culture, Eurasians formulated and established principles of their own sociopolitical and economic program. The soviet system, freed from an ideological doctrinaire attitude, was recognized by them as the best state form. They believed that the soviet system in its authentic form would ensure people's democracy and the selection and promotion of the most suitable people for office. The federal principle of the union, according to them, was to be kept. The USSR was to become a fraternal union of the peoples who inhabit Eurasia. Its principle was to be a supranational system built on national foundations.

We should note that this was said and written in 1927, when communism and the Soviet Union were associated mainly with the ardent speeches of Trotsky, who considered soviets to be only a temporary, historically caused form of the dictatorship of the proletariat. But the Eurasian worldview, aimed primarily at revealing Russia's uniqueness, considered soviets to be a permanent form of national self-government for Russia. In this connection, the Spanish philosopher Ortega y Gasset observed in 1930: "Moscow is covering itself with a thin veil of European ideas, that is, with Marxism, which was created in Europe with reference to European issues and problems. Under this veil live people who differ from Europe not only ethnically but, more importantly, by their age—they are a young nation that has not yet been leavened. If Marxism were to win out in Russia, where there is no industry, this would be the greatest paradox that could befall Marxism."[36]

In arriving at this conclusion, he proceeded from the simple observation that the development of a capitalist economy inevitably fragments society, in which the key role begins to be played by the atomized person. But the Soviet people remained a people of a traditional Eurasian society. And by the end of the 1920s, the Russian worldview had "digested" and adapted Marxist ideology to fit its own culture. The same thing took place later in China.

To understand the condition of Russia at a crossroad today, we must compare the fundamental categories characterizing the way of life and the worldview of Eurasia with those of Europe. Europe is supposedly the only possible "world civilization," to which we all should return. This civilization has been vividly depicted by such Western scholars as Nietzsche, Weber, Spengler, and Hayek. A time-portrait of Russia has been drawn by Fyodor Dostoevsky, Dmitry Mendeleev, Georgy Vernadsky, and the Eurasians. But the "modernizers" of Russia who want to drag our people into a market economy present a vulgarized and "enhanced" caricature of European civilization. They are totally insensitive to the drama of the West. As was noted by the Eurasians, the same was true of their predecessors. For example, Georges Florovsky wrote about the Russian Westernizers of seventy years ago: "Their seeming admiration for Europe only covers up their deep inattention to and disrespect for its tragic destiny."

Here we must limit ourselves to a sketchy comparison of these two civilizations as they really are:

Assumptions About the Person and the People

Modern Western civilization is based on an atomist-mechanical picture of the world. The traditional bonds uniting people in a patriarchal society were cast off under the slogan: "Each person is a free atom of humankind!" A marketplace individualism became the basis of man's worldview and his economic and political ("one person—one vote") assumptions. Hence the absolutization of individual rights, which in the national sphere justified melting smaller nationalities into larger nations and in the social sphere stood for competition—a "war of all against all."

In Russia, such a complete atomization has not taken place, even over the past seventy-five years. The individual continues to feel part of a collective structure of one type or another—a labor collective, a collective farm, or a brigade. (Alexander Yakovlev thus writes angrily: "We need willpower and wisdom gradually to destroy the Bolshevik community—the collective farm. . . . Here there can be no compromise . . . decollectivization must be conducted lawfully but forcefully.") The most important spiritual category for Eurasians is the people [the nation], which is rejected by our Westernizers. The perception of the people as a single organism, a sort of social microcosm, was formulated by the Eurasian L. Karsavin as follows: "One can speak about a body of people. . . . My biological organism is a concrete process, my concrete interaction with other organisms and with nature. . . . A nation living in a given territory is the same kind of organism (only it is supraindividual). It has its own body."

It is obvious how much this cultural-historical concept contradicts the Western model of the individual that underlies the Yeltsin–Gaidar reforms. This fact causes such uncontrollable rage among the defenders of a market democracy that they even forget elementary civility. For example, Yury Buyda recently wrote in *The Independent Gazette*: "The opposition to a market is an attribute of the traditional [Russian] mentality that is tied to a "communal" economy. . . . Our economic deformity still makes it possible to exploit more or less effectively the myth about us as some communality united by blood, soil, and fate, for real human ties are still in their rudimentary stage and will attain strength only in a multilayer, atomized society." Answering a foreign correspondent about the character of these strong new "ties" toward which we are all imagined to aspire, the poet Iosif Brodsky used one word: "Money."[37] And these lofty "aspirations" are being imposed on Russia!

The concept of the person as an atom breaks the great, time-honored tie of generations and takes Europe's suicidal society of selfish consumption to be the ideal.

Against this, the sacred concept of "the people" presupposes a most profound responsibility to the dead and their descendants. Today, we would be frightened of meeting the shadows of our fathers and grandfathers; as we were warned after February 1917 by one of the contributors to *Landmarks*:[38]

> The dead are silent. . . . Nevertheless, this army of the dead is a great— one could say the greatest—political force of our entire life. They died and live transformed in the people's soul. There, in that new profound life, they have indissolubly merged with the cause and the faith for the sake of which they perished; their souls speak distinctly only about the Motherland, about the protection of the state, about the honor and dignity of the country; about the beauty of heroic deeds and about the shame of treason. They complain about deliberate and unintentional acts of betrayal, about democratized pillage, about senseless and unscrupulous feasting on their graves, about the plunder of their native land, soaked with their blood. Let us respect the shadows of the dead in our national soul.

Assumptions About the Country and the State

The atomized individual of the West, being the carrier of "personal rights," is incorporated through spontaneous market forces into civil society. He regards the state as merely a "night watchman" of the market with rather limited functions. The old empires have broken up into small "nation-states," which today are integrated through economic ties. Eurasia, however, with its unique continental landscape, has traveled a totally different road. Here, the state was given the sacred status of "father" (if sometimes an unduly strict father), not a "servant." Georgy V. Vernadsky noted that "the ties of the people with the state formed by this people and with the space inhabited by this people, with its development, are not accidental." And Pavel Savitsky explains it in more detail:

> The unique, supremely precise and at the same time simple geographic structure of Russia-Eurasia is related to a number of major geopolitical circumstances. The nature of the Eurasian world is minimally favorable for various kinds of "separatism"—whether political, cultural, or eco-

nomic.... Ethnic and cultural elements have [here] gone through an intensive interaction, cross-breeding, and mixing.... It is no accident that the spirit of a "brotherhood of nations" hovers over Eurasia, which has its origins in many centuries of contacts and cultural mergers of various peoples.... The "will to join together for a common cause" can be easily awakened here. In this way, the Russian Empire, the USSR, and earlier the Scythian, the Hun, and the Mongol Empires were established. Thus emerged the unique, distinctive coexistence of cultures that the Eurasians call a "rainbow" or a "symphony."

This historical fact, which the Eurasians explained with their linguistic findings (Nikolai Trubetskoy) and their terrain research (Pavel Savitsky), is totally rejected by their current opponents—the "democrats." As Algis Prazauskas, a writer for *The Independent Gazette*, noted, Russia and the USSR are a "unique Eurasian panopticum of peoples who have nothing in common except clan properties and artificially created disasters." But then how can you explain that at the beginning of the century there were about 1.5 million Armenians in Russia, and they lived safely until perestroika and created a strong and modern state. There used to be about 2.5 million Armenians in Turkey, and now there are only 100,000; they have lost their national self-awareness to such an extent that they even deny the genocide suffered by their own people in 1915.

The "last Eurasian" (as he called himself), Lev Gumilyov, noticed a very important link in Eurasian ideology: "The nationalism of each separate nation in Eurasia (USSR) must be combined with all-Eurasian nationalism." This explains why there were no destructive flare-ups of aggressive, egotistical nationalism in the USSR. Local nationalisms were strongly linked with a great-power consciousness, Eurasian "all-union" patriotism, and all-Eurasian nationalism. For example, an inhabitant of Nagorno-Karabakh [a region in the Caucasus contested between Armenia and Azerbaijan—Ed.] felt himself to be above all a citizen of the USSR, and the very idea of a war between Armenia and Azerbaijan was absurd to him. But after the USSR was seriously weakened and the "imperial Eurasian" consciousness was ideologically discredited, local nationalism, now released from the bonds of union power, began to tear the country apart.

The Eurasian character of the Soviet Union made each of its parts "neither Europe nor Asia" and synthesized and combined its various cultural genotypes. Soviet Tajiks and Kazakhs, although living in Asia, were also Europeans. Perhaps Tajik students, overtaken by "democratic" intoxication, failed to realize what it would really mean to "break up Eurasianism," but their advisers in the USSR Academy of Sciences and in overseas academies knew perfectly well what was going to happen. Central Asia is a complex ethnic world, which has been developing in its own civilized way. The strong influence of clan and family relations often resulted in collisions and local wars. This changed when the Central Asian peoples were integrated into the Eurasian geopolitical space. In this manner, "absorbing rods" were inserted into their ethnic reactor. By joint efforts, a refined, flexible mechanism for quelling conflicts was created and used. Clans that were hostile to each other were separated by Russian fortresses and garrisons, disputed areas were seized by the state treasury, food and even water supplies were regulated to keep excessively militant princes in check, and so forth. During the Soviet era, these methods were augmented by the work of soviets, intermediaries from regional Party structures, personnel selection, bonuses, medals, and so on. Why did all this come to a sudden end? Why did the army garrisons begin to look indifferently at the destruction of children, women, and the elderly? Entire regions found themselves thrown outside the bounds of civilization and pushed to the verge of destruction.

There have been many attempts to destroy the Eurasian bonds of the USSR and Russia. When our "Chicago boys"[39] proudly declare that they are true Westernizers who are consciously following the Western (more correctly, the Anglo-Saxon) version of capitalism, we should recall that their main slogan, which dates back to the 1960s and is being used to destroy the whole Eurasian civilization of Russia, called for the dissolution of the Slavic-Turkic symbiosis and the "return" of Russians to the "European home." Had this idea been implemented, it would have thrown Russia out of the Urals and even out of the Volga region. Peter Vail and Alexander Genis, emigrants from the USSR, demonstrated this in their book *The '60s. The World of Soviet Man.*[40]

The authors describe how the dispute about our attitude toward the Western influence on Russia became a war for the values of world civilization. It was no longer a question of different directions or various schools of thought but of Russia's historical place on the map of humankind. Ilya Ehrenburg became the ideologist and prophet of this new kind of Westernism (Vail and Genis likened him to the Apostle

Paul).[41] According to them, "I. Ehrenburg passionately argued that the Russians were neither better nor worse than the West simply because they were part of the West." In those years, after the space flight of Yury Gagarin, the appeal to give up our burdensome union with the "Tatars" and to transform the "Asian" component of the USSR into a well-controlled internal "third world" was presented in a flattering wrapping (what a contrast to today's mocking!). Vail and Genis wrote: "What I. Ehrenburg wanted to tell us, and did tell us, is very simple: Russia is part of Europe. . . . Indeed, what can divide such remarkable peoples? Only trifles." Today, there is no more courting of Russians, and the liberals are vying with each other to prove that Russians are not and could never have been Europeans because they chose Orthodoxy and preferred the Asian inhabitants of the steppe to the cultured Teutonic knights. Partly as a result of such ideas, we can now be accepted into "world civilization" only on the rigid conditions of the International Monetary Fund.

Today, the destruction of our country and the demolition of its Eurasian base are being accomplished not only by splitting apart ethnic unions and fueling national separatism. Nations and ethnic groups themselves are being split along all possible fractures (including even schisms within religious denominations).

An important goal of the "democrats" today is to split apart the uniform body of the Russian people and undermine the "communal spirit" that, although not even mentioned for seventy-five years, in reality united us so firmly (as the Great Patriotic War proved). At the beginning of the century, an earlier attempt to destroy us as an entity through class antagonism led to an almost fatal catastrophe. And now, already spent class antagonisms are being artificially rekindled. A major task of the reform, we are told, is the "formation of a new class of private proprietors." Can you imagine a more ideologized task? The emergence of this class by revolutionary expropriation at the expense of the working people rather than by natural accumulation of capital over time through entrepreneurial activity will inevitably result in social and political disaster. And this process is being expedited by creating an artificial cultural confrontation between generations.

To disunite Russians, ideologists are trying to convince them that they do not represent one nation but are divided into two very different subspecies. Just read the "democratic" newspapers, which are calling for a new civil war in which "two nations will fight: the new Russians and the old Russians—those who can adapt to this new epoch, and those who are incapable of doing so." This is the main idea of our new spiritual shepherds. Judging by the behavior of our teenagers and youth and the words of their favorite songs, this propaganda has in many respects been successful. Young people today see themselves as "new Russians." They think they can adapt to the new epoch—they need only not be afraid to settle accounts with the old Russians who are blocking the way. This notion once before led to a "Russia washed in blood." Let every mother who has heartfelt ties with her son remember this.

Today, the creative assimilation of the ideas of Eurasianism, which for many reasons are disquieting for nationalists, patriots of the "white idea," and communists alike, can serve as the path to reconciliation and is the right response to those who would reopen our old wounds and again set whites against reds, Russians against Tatars, Christians against Moslems. In this effort, we should expect attempts at sabotage by those politicians who hate Eurasianism in all its basic aspects and who may even mask themselves as Eurasians. But life is quickly teaching us to overcome our blindness and credulity. Both our scholarly knowledge and our innate feeling for our Motherland will help us to understand this. All we need to do is use our brains and listen to our hearts, as was recently done at the Congress of the National Salvation Front, where a historical reconciliation of those who had been divided by the terrible year 1917 took place.

The Russian Question

Let us be frank: the slowness of today's Russian patriotic consciousness is its main defect. If the patriotic movement in Russia is to survive and if its leaders are serious about saving our state, it is necessary to make an urgent effort to develop an ideology for national revival that is wholesome, comprehensive, and effective in practice. It is on the basis of such an ideology that the strategy and tactics of the national-liberation movement should then be developed. This is our only chance to wrest the initiative from the hands of those who hate Russia.

What has taken place in Russia in recent years has not been accidental. Only a completely naive person could believe that these events have been the result of our country's "natural development."

It is our duty to formulate in a simple, accessible form answers to the major questions of the day: Who is destroying Russia? How is this being done and why? And, most importantly, what should be done to oppose this betrayal?

Acquiring a harmonious, sensible, and universally acceptable philosophy cannot be simple and easy. False stereotypes have been deliberately embedded in the public consciousness to divert our attention from the reality of events. Skillfully designed by Russophobic ideologists, these stereotypes have for many years prevented us from impartially and sensibly comprehending what has been occurring all around us. For this reason it is necessary to state honestly that this will be difficult for us to do. Many of us will have to abandon our favorite illusions and dogmas and accept new realities, which can sometimes be very bitter and disturbing. We will also have to learn how to assess the world on our own and to act with initiative, quickly, and resolutely.

Who Is Destroying Russia?

Many of our readers will simply say: "Why do you even ask? This is certainly the handiwork of the unscrupulous and shameless regime of politicians and grabbers that established itself on the ruins of the Soviet Empire."

But some more sophisticated readers will remark: "It is not that simple. Yeltsin and company could never have stayed in power after all they have done to Russia were it not for the powerful and extensive support of the West. Strictly speaking, Yeltsin can hardly be considered an independent political figure. He is a puppet whose strings are being pulled from across the ocean. America, our main geopolitical opponent, has become the indisputable world leader. America is the real source of hostile influence."

The most thoughtful readers may add further arguments: "But even the United States is not quite independent. Look more closely. This is not a traditional state but an overgrown commercial-industrial corporation. As such, it has no national interests but hides under this term the interests of an international financial oligarchy. This worldwide corporation uses the political, military, and economic power of America as an instrument to achieve mercenary interests and purposes. The cosmopolitan elite of international capital is the real behind-the-scenes orchestrator of Russia's troubles."

All three answers are no doubt correct. Yet all three are also insufficient and incomplete. The regime of the "Yeltsinoids" is a brief passing episode in the life of Russia. Deprived of any significant intellectual resources, it cannot pursue an intelligent policy, except for the Kremlin's court intrigues and the mercenary interests of the corrupt bureaucracy. The source of the influences that are so pernicious for Russia is to be sought much deeper.

An analysis of the position of the United States and the West in relation to the "Russian question" provides the best starting point. The many centuries of military, religious, political, and economic rivalry between Russia and Western Europe clearly show the differences between our own and the West's public and state values, cultures, and historically formed national worldviews. There is much about us that the West does not understand. It is afraid of our state power. It is in the interests of the West to weaken, divide, and economically enslave Russia.

More than a thousand years of failed efforts to eliminate Russia from the historical arena should have proved to the West the futility of this approach. Besides, the material prosperity and unlimited consumption that have been raised by Western civilization to a rank of the highest value require international stability, which from time immemorial has been ensured only by a balance of powers. For the sake of its own peace and quiet, the West is now ready to accept the existence of a national Russian state.

For the same reasons, international capital, although interested in the total economic weakening of Russia and its elimination from the world stage as a dangerous trade competitor, has every reason to avoid the cataclysms that would inevitably ensue if the Russian geopolitical space were to disintegrate.

Nevertheless, all these structures—the political regime established on the territory of Russia, Western states, and transnational banking-financial corporations—are all vehicles of an aggressive and irreconcilable anti-Russian policy. In the modern world, an independent Russia is the main obstacle to the creation of a "new world order," which would entail the formation of supranational bodies of political, economic, and military leadership.

This delusion of absolute power has a long history, closely related to the development of secret political societies, obscure religious sects, and mystical cults. But only now, at the end of the twentieth century, has it become possible to make it a reality.

Only with a realization of this danger can the purposefulness and clarity of the patriotic movement's activity be fully appreciated and given the needed popular support.

How Is Russia Being Destroyed?

To answer this question, we need to analyze the technology of power behind the flimsy facade of Russian "democracy."

First, we will find that there are both real and illusory centers of power. We will see a persistent tendency to hide the mechanisms of real power from the eyes of outsiders by concealing them under various official structures and simultaneously to transform the latter into obedient executors of decisions made in advance. The manipulators are consistently trying, and not without success, to make the system of state power in Russia into an "executive" machine capable only of blindly implementing concepts that have been worked out by persons unknown in places unknown.

Second, we must appreciate the fact that there is a secret hierarchy of authority that is not the official chain of command of the formal bodies of state power or the notorious "executive vertical" but rather a behind-the-scenes network of agents who have "decisive influence" in all areas of Russian life.

At the bottom of this hierarchy is its most primitive tool, the power structure of physical force. It is used if needed, but, as the events of May 1 [1993] in Moscow demonstrated,[42] it is likely to provoke retaliatory reactions and thus cannot solve the problems facing the regime. Moreover, history unambiguously confirms that it is impossible to destroy Russia by force alone.

The next level is represented by the power of economic compulsion, which in its effects, if not by intention, has already acquired some characteristics of a planned genocide. Economic compulsion makes it possible to program people's behavior by creating certain kinds of socioeconomic relations. This power is more flexible and effective than open violence and is less conspicuous. People do not immediately realize that the problems of survival and the programmed terms of their solutions sharply limit their freedom of choice, making a large part of their behavior and consciousness subject to "decisive influences" from outside. However, at present this economic instrument of power lacks the needed technological precision.

Political power has more precision and universality and hence offers broader opportunities. It has the ability to program the "rules of the game" for the systems of the state and society. By modifying these rules in accordance with its own ultimate goals, the conductors can achieve any desired result within an acceptable range of probability.

The highest form of power, undoubtedly, is conceptual—the power of ideological programming based on the technology of purposefully constructing a worldview and the fundamental values of personal, family, community, and state life.

In this construction, the stereotypes of public consciousness (ideals) that do not fit the given program must be destroyed and replaced by new "values" that accommodate the needs of the "programmer" and carry a predetermined philosophical code. The main concern here is to conceal these actions thoroughly and present them as the "natural course of events."

Now we are ready to review the technologies used for the destruction of Russia.

In ideology, these are the destruction of our spiritual roots; the disruption of the Russian historical tradition; the discrediting of commonly accepted state, religious, moral, and other philosophical values; the cultivation of individualism; the propagation of Western mass culture; the deprivation of a national identity; the promotion of hostility; and the encouragement of human passions and vices. The ultimate goal is clearly the destruction of our national self-awareness.

In politics, the ancient principle "divide and conquer" is being practiced in its modern version. In economics, the goal is to integrate our national economy into the global economic system as a peripheral structure incapable of independent existence by breaking up the unified national economic complex, denationalizing property, concentrating on the priority development of raw-materials and extraction branches, and suffocating high-technology industries and fundamental sciences.

What Can We Do to Oppose Russia's Destroyers?

In ideology, we have to achieve a precise and clear comprehension of our supreme national task. For centuries Russia has considered itself destined to show the world the treasures of the human spirit as reflected in personal life, family traditions, the social system, and the form of the state. Over many centuries, this idea has taken on diverse philosophical, religious, and ideological forms. It inspired the creators of the universal formula "Moscow as the Third Rome," expressed in the severe, courageous, and ascetic colors of Russian Orthodoxy. Later, garbed in the trinity of the Russian Empire's motto—"Orthodoxy, Autocracy, Nationality"—this idea rallied under the majestic arch of the Russian state the "score of tongues" forming the unified family of Russian nations.

Fighters for the nation's happiness were inspired by it, and after October 1917 its life-giving breath kept the national soul together in spite of ideologists of a "permanent revolution"—cynical cosmopolitans who looked upon Russia only as a base for instigating a worldwide conflagration. It helped us to get through times of cold and famine, destruction, and hostile international actions. It helped us achieve a glorious victory in a most bloody war and then re-create that great power on the ruins of which renegades, traitors, and Russophobes are feasting today.

We have now reached a decisive moment. By restoring the Russian idea in all its historical greatness and spiritual power and enriching it with our recent tragic and heroic experiences, we can at last reunite our dismembered historical Fatherland, cure its illnesses, mend its fractures, and heal the ulcers of national self-awareness.

In politics, we must rally around the ideology of Russia's revival to create, as soon as possible, a practical and effective mechanism for coordinating the interests and actions of all patriotic forces within the framework of a unified national-salvation movement.

We should agree about our understanding of a multiparty system as a tool for realizing the social, ethical, economic, and religious aspects of the unified national idea. For centuries, this concept was based on two premises. First, a powerful state was the main guarantor of the free and historically continuous development of society. And second, the basic purpose of this development was the maximally complete implementation of our traditional social, state, family, and moral-ethical ideals.

Within the framework of this ideology of Russia's revival, there will be a place for everyone: supporters of the principles of social justice, adherents of the idea of a law-based state, Orthodox and Moslem believers, and those who express the expectations of the working class, the peasantry, and the intelligentsia. And we should firmly tell those who would provoke confrontation, discord, and division: "It will not work, gentlemen!" The convergence of the deep, historically formed interests that bind our society into a unique and original organism—political, economical, spiritual, cultural, and religious—is more important and more substantial than the short-term tactical interests of various ethnic and professional groups, social strata, and ideological movements of today.

Now we must mention the interests of the "fifth column," the "agents of influence" who are promoting the "new world order." This small but extremely active group cannot be considered a natural factor in Russia's political life but is rather the product of the purposeful activity of forces openly hostile to basic Russian interests. The unconditional removal of this group from power should be the first step on our way to normalizing life in our country.

Questions of concrete political activity are not within the scope of this work. In conclusion, I would like to repeat: today we cannot afford to be lazy in our thinking or slow in our comprehension of the new realities. We are simply obligated—it is our duty to our people—to wrest our country away from the designers of a global political dictatorship and return it to the path of our historically continuous, harmonious development!

A New World Order

Since World War II, the scientific revolution has brought humankind to the very technological edge of gaining comprehensive global control over its own development. Today's information systems can already effectively coordinate all the essential aspects—ideological, political, economic, demographic, and ecological—of the development of human civilization.

It is therefore not surprising that we are witnessing today the extensive activation of transnational, cosmopolitan forces, which see this as a real opportunity to give concrete geopolitical form to their dream of a world superstate. The authors of one-world schemes believe that their supranational structure, once established, will gradually absorb all national sovereign states. Large powers will first be subjected to internally stimulated processes of disintegration and will then be broken up into smaller pieces that can be more easily "digested." The bottom line calls for all countries, as they continue to lose their independence, to be subsumed into a field of universal political influence and turned into peripheral entities and "relay stations" for the directives of a single governing center. Practical efforts to create such a center have been going on for a long time.

What are the consequences of all this for Russia? In very general terms, they may be summarized as follows.

First, in the economic sphere, we are today more certain than ever that the world's reserves of raw materials are far from infinite. In fact, they are quite limited, allowing us to calculate that any attempt by Russia or the developing countries to reach, for example, the level of energy consumption that supports the high living standards of the "golden billion" in the so-called "developed" countries is doomed to failure. Any such attempt would lead to an enormous global economic crisis and ecological catastrophe. To ensure harmonious worldwide development, the West must accept self-imposed limitations. This is the only way to bridge the gap between a handful of superrich countries and the rest of humankind. Needless to say, the West considers such a solution unacceptable, at least in the near future. And it is precisely for this reason that the developed capitalist countries support the idea of establishing a "new world order" (NWO), within the framework of which they hope to be able to retain their privileged leading positions.

With this in mind, the model of a united world economy within the NWO framework envisages different levels of consumption for different components of the system. Certain regions would continue to prosper, while the development of other regions would be artificially frozen. Need we bother to conjecture in which category Russia would end up under this "division of labor"?

Second, in the military-political sphere, the unevenness of living standards will continue to be a source of justifiable, endless conflicts. And the use of military power will be required to localize and suppress them. The so-called "carpet bombings" in Iraq and the punitive raids of the "blue helmets" in virtually occupied Mogadishu demonstrated the degree of cynicism and cruelty that the "international community" is willing to accept in this connection. Small as it is, Serbia has so far managed to escape a similar fate only thanks to the heroic resistance of its entire nation.

In 1993 alone, the United Nations undertook more than ten "peacekeeping" operations. In 1994, the total number of international "peacemaking" forces will far exceed 100,000 troops. It is significant that there have already been several calls for their use in the territories of the former republics of the USSR. There is reason to believe that, since the liquidation of the Soviet Union, the role of the United Nations has rapidly been changing from that of the harmonizer of international relations and to that of a tool to put in place a geopolitical dictatorship.

The consequences of these developments are especially dangerous for us, because the regime of national betrayal now in power in Russia will most likely become an obedient agent of foreign influence in the event of a state of emergency in our country. It is easy to see why: our self-appointed pseudo-elite of unprincipled power mongers and corrupt nouveaux riches is tempted by the opportunity to be admitted into the transnational ruling class—the new masters of the world, who are holding the steering wheel of the "international community"—even if it has to crawl on its belly to do so.

Third, in the national-cultural and spiritual sphere, it is not possible to govern humankind from a single center without first achieving maximum unification and standardization. To do this, all the local specific features of the countries subjected to control must be minimized. In plain language, this means that the national and cultural uniqueness of various peoples, as well as their spiritual, historical, and religious originality, would be in danger of complete annihilation.

Accordingly, as is already being done in Russia, measures would have to be taken to impose "universal human values" on everyone without exception. In the area of religious life, for example, the prospects of this activity are tied to the ecumenical movement and in the area of culture to rampant commercialization.

Ethnic diversity and regional demography would also be subjected to unification efforts. Nations judged to have an unpromising future or to exceed numerical limits as determined by projections of minimal consumption would be subjected to planned reductions. This could easily be done by regulating living conditions—there is no need for concentration camps and gas chambers. At least in Russia, population growth figures have declined two years in a row. This is a concrete example of how economic "reforms" can be used to regulate demographic processes.

What awaits us in the immediate future? In principle, we have two choices under existing conditions. First, we can accept the rules of the game that are being imposed upon us and then fight to expand our essential "quotas" within the blueprints for universal world development. This would mean reconciling ourselves to the loss of political and economic sovereignty, to the irreversible destruction of a millennium of Russian spirituality and culture, to flagrant social injustice, and to the transformation of our country into a launching pad for the "new world order." In exchange for this, we would be given the opportunity for a majority of us to survive biologically; for a select, "qualified" minority to live decently; and for the compradorian elite, in its role as trusted overseers of their own compatriots, to enjoy world-class luxury.

The second choice assumes that Russia would stand up to the historic challenge our people face today. In this case, we would refuse to reconcile ourselves to the prospect of enslavement and would try to regain for our country our former role as a great power. Russia would again strive to harmonize different national-political interests, preserve a balance of power in the world, ensure a diversity of patterns of development, and prevent geopolitical monopoly by any nation.

In essence, this is a question of the life or death of our state. Of foremost importance today is our struggle for national liberation. All ideological differences are overshadowed by this struggle. Today, two parties are confronting each other in Russia: the party of "this country" and the party of "our country." Let us not lose time floundering. Let us act while our future is still in our hands!

Editor's Notes

1. Sam Keen, *Faces of the Enemy* (San Francisco: Harper and Row, 1991).
2. This is the title of a poem by Vladimir Mayakovsky (1893–1930).
3. The Molotov–Ribbentrop agreement (1939) had secret protocols concerning the Baltic States. For some fifty years Moscow denied the existence of these documents.
4. Mikhail Saltykov-Shchedrin (1826–1889) was a Russian satirical writer.
5. These are the names of prominent scientists and political figures.
6. This is the title of a one-act play by Alexander Pushkin (1799–1837).
7. These were a tank and a self-propelled gun made in World War II Germany.
8. Sergei Korolyov (1907–1966) was a pioneer of the Soviet space-rocket industry.
9. *Okhrana*, or colloquially *okhranka*, was the secret police in tsarist Russia.
10. These were officials of the Central Committee of the CPSU.
11. "Instructors" were middle-ranking party officials; "secretaries" were higher-ranking party officials. The latter were nominally elected to their offices.
12. The reference here is to a controversial effort to consolidate small depopulated villages. The effort was aborted.

13. The reference here is to the first plenary meeting of the Central Committee of the newly established (1990) Communist Party of Russia as a branch of the CPSU.

14. All came to national prominence as members of the Congress of People's Deputies elected in 1989 and as participants in the resistance to the August 1991 coup. Gavril Popov is a noted economist who served as the first post-Soviet mayor of Moscow. Telman Gdlyan rose to fame for exposing official corruption. Galina Starovoitova championed the rights of national minorities. Marina Salye was a people's deputy from St. Petersburg.

15. During 1991, there were many unsuccessful attempts to create a diminished version of the Soviet Union and thus to prevent its approaching collapse. Gorbachev's plan for a Union of Sovereign States was drafted at his dacha in Novo-Ogarevo, outside Moscow; but the treaty signing planned for August 1991 never took place. The Commonwealth of Independent States was conceived at the early December 1991 meeting of the presidents of Russia (Yeltsin), Ukraine (Kravchuk), and Belarus (Shushkevich) at Belovezh Forest, outside Minsk.

16. Lenin's New Economic Policy (NEP) was introduced in 1921. It called for a mixed socialist-capitalist economy. The NEP was phased out by Stalin by the end of the 1920s.

17. Eduard Shevardnadze was a close associate of Gorbachev's during the initial years of perestroika. He is now president of Georgia.

18. A niece of Peter the Great's, Anna Ivanovna ruled Russia from 1730 to 1740.

19. Alexander Yanov has written several books and articles on Russian authoritarianism. More recently he has compared the Yeltsin regime with the failed Weimar Republic in Germany.

20. Nikolai Karamzin (1766–1826), a writer and historian, served as tutor to the future Emperor Alexander I.

21. Georgy Zhukov (1896–1974) and Nikolai Vatutin (1901–1944) were famous military leaders in World War II; Yevgeny Paton (1870–1953) was a prominent scientist and engineer. For Korolyov, see note 8.

22. Andrei Vyshinsky (1883–1954) was Stalin's favorite prosecutor of "enemies of the people." Lavrenty Beria (1899–1953) and Genrikh Yagoda (1891–1938) were chiefs of Stalin's secret police.

23. *Moscow News* and *Ogonyok* were the most radical pro-perestroika periodicals during the 1980s.

24. General Igor Rodionov was appointed Russia's defense minister in July 1996.

25. When he commanded the 14th Army stationed in Moldova, General Alexander Lebed and his troops protected the Russian enclave, the self-proclaimed Trans-Dniester Republic. After the USSR collapsed, Russians feared that Moldova would seek to unite with Romania.

26. This is the title of Boris Yeltsin's autobiography.

27. Vladimir Kirshon (1902–1938) was a noted playwrite. Alexei Losev (1893–1986) was a philosopher.

28. From December 1992, when the Supreme Soviet rejected the appointment of Yegor Gaidar as prime minister, Yeltsin was on a collision course with the Russian parliament, culminating in the October shootout. New elections and a referendum on a new Constitution were held in December 1993.

29. Ivan Bunin (1870–1953) and Mikhail Sholokhov (1905–1984) were Nobel Prize laureates in literature. Bunin emigrated from Russia after the 1917 revolution.

30. Komsomol stands for the Communist Youth League.

31. General Anton Denikin (1872–1947) was one of the top leaders of the White armies during the 1918–21 civil war in Russia.

32. Nikolai Berdyaev (1874–1948) was a Russian religious philosopher. He left Russia after the 1917 revolution and lived for some thirty years in France.

33. Valentin Rasputin is a popular Russian writer who is actively involved in various nationalist-patriotic organizations. Sergei Baburin is a prominent political leader of the younger generation who opposed the dissolution of the Soviet Union. General Boris Gromov, is popularly regarded as a strong defender of Russian interests. Ramazan Abdulatipov was chairman of the Russian Federation's Soviet of Nationalities.

34. *Exodus to the East* was published in Sofia, Bulgaria, in 1921.

35. By 1930, all the activities of the promoters of Eurasian ideas in the Soviet Union were banned. Many members of the movement were arrested and exiled to Siberia. More recently their ideas were popularized by the late ethnologist Lev Gumilyov (1912–1993), son of the poets Nikolai Gumilyov and Anna Akhmatova, who spent much of his early life in the Gulag.

36. José Ortega y Gasset (1883–1955) was a noted Spanish philosopher. He frequently visited the Soviet Union.

37. Joseph (Iosif) Brodsky (1940–1995) was a Nobel Prize–winning Russian poet. He was expelled from the Soviet Union and lived the last twenty years of his life in the United States.

38. The *Vekhi* (*Landmarks*) anthology was published by a group of liberal intellectuals in 1909 including Nikolai Berdyaev, Sergei Bulgakov, and five others.

39. Reference is to economic reformers influenced be the "Chicago School."

40. *The '60s. The World of Soviet Man* was written in Russian by the émigrés Alexander Genis and Peter Vail in the 1980s.

41. Ilya Ehrenburg (1891–1967) was a major Soviet writer and journalist.

42. Reference is to a May Day demonstration that ended in a confrontation with police.

Part 3

Russia and the Contemporary World

Let Russia Be Russia

This material was written for various newspapers and magazines between late 1993 and 1995, when it was published as a book. During this time, Zyuganov was organizing and consolidating his opposition movement, which was built around the Communist Party and included both left (socialist) and right (nationalist) parties and groups.

—V.M.

At a Crossroads

I

All honest people looking at current conditions in our country and society understand that a dangerous limit has been reached and that a way out of this crisis must be found. But in our search for a solution, we must remember that each person has a set of values of paramount importance: culture, spirituality, safety, health, concern for the territorial integrity of our country, the opportunity for worthy democratic activity, and many others. It is obvious today that the ideology of liberalism has suffered a shattering defeat in Russia, and this has resulted in disaster, tragedy, and in many regions violence, war, and outright genocide.

A difficult and intensive search for a way out of the impasse is taking place. It is as if Ilya Muromets were standing at the intersection of three roads:[1] one road, if followed, would transform our entire country into a vast Chechnya. This "bloodbath formula" is completely unacceptable even to the most radical and irrational minds. The second road would lead to the transformation of our country into a magnified Colombia, where politics and the mafia merge and the latter is radically politicized. The outlines of such a state already exist—the readiness to engage in unlimited repression inside our country and the willingness to use nuclear blackmail outside it. Those currently in power in the Kremlin have no moral brakes or ethical constraints. The third road calls for democratic development on the basis of the Russian national state philosophy, high spiritual values, and a historical tradition that could bring together the past and the present, creating a worthy future for our people.

The philosopher Ivan Ilin wrote: "In thinking about Russia's future and preparing it in our minds, we should proceed from its historical, national, religious, cultural, and state foundations and interests. We should not dare to sell out or squander our common Russian national wealth. We should not dare to promise on behalf of Russia any part of her to anyone. We should remember Russia and only Russia. We should be faithful to it and only to it. Any generation of Russians that behaves differently will be branded in the history of Russia as a feeble and traitorous generation."[2]

I am sure that most of our country's responsible citizens would not like to be known as a feeble, much less a traitorous, generation. Given that assumption, the creation of a union of national-patriotic forces nowadays acquires special meaning. We see that union's role, above all, in conducting elections at all three levels: local, parliamentary, and presidential. Working with a very wide range of patriotic forces, we should prepare a joint program acceptable to our country, our nation, and our multinational society. This program should represent the future interests of everyone who lives within our country and should respect the rights of our neighbors.

II

The problems of Russia's development and formation have always been at the center of attention of Russian philosophical thinking, the intelligentsia's ideological disputes, and the general public's political passions. These problems become especially urgent at critical moments in our fatherland's history, which occur with a frequency that is not characteristic of other nations. During such moments, the highest surges of state power and spiritual purity alternate with periods of political disaster and religious-moral chaos. To survive such times, the path of development we choose and the ways we use to achieve socially meaningful goals and to resolve problems that have an impact on the fate of our country not only at present but also in the foreseeable future are particularly vital.

Socialism in its Russian form promoted the preservation of the integrity of the state and its transformation into a world power. The sociopolitical system that developed allowed us to bring about major changes in manufacturing, education, science, medical care, housing, guaranteed rest and recreation, and the enjoyment of cultural treasures. And these changes were made in the shortest period recorded in world history for such a transformation. A powerful army equipped with modern weapons was created, and significant successes in foreign policy were achieved. But, as we well know, the Russian form of socialism had serious defects. These flaws might have been removed. However, for a number of reasons, this was not done.

Consequently, in the 1970s and 1980s, the national economy of the USSR began to display signs of stagnation. This occurred because the rigid system of state ownership of all property, including so-called "cooperative ownership," stifled incentives in commerce and manufacturing, delayed the introduction of new technologies, and destroyed the motivation to work.

Monopolistic state ownership contributed to the creation of a rigid political system, which by the end of the 1980s encompassed the Communist Party of the Soviet Union (CPSU), various bodies of soviet power, trade unions, power ministries, the ministry of foreign affairs, and the industrial and agrarian complexes. A virtual merging of party and state had taken place, permeated by a uniform ideology. Thus, a consummate political-managerial system throttling any attempts to change the status quo was developed, with self-preservation as its basic function.

Attempts to change the rigidity of this system did manifest themselves from time to time, initiated by such political leaders as Nikita Khrushchev, Alexei Kosygin, and especially Yuri Andropov.[3] However, these attempts, with the possible exception of Kosygin's efforts, were within the framework of the existing ideological and administrative system.

Nevertheless, the country's intellectual and material potential for change was accumulating. Eventually, it could no longer be contained within the framework of the established political structure. Society was inevitably moving closer to the line beyond which change becomes unavoidable. Gradually, all public institutions found themselves in a slowly progressing paralysis, which became known as the "era of stagnation." The functioning of processes in every sphere of life in our country at that time was impeded. Attempts to overcome this stagnation during the perestroika period by accelerating socioeconomic development and introducing political reforms did not lead to the desired results.

During perestroika, the search for remedies included the ideology of renewal, which, with its emphasis on the communality of human values, promoted the humanization of ideological activity and an improved dialectical understanding of the current reality and expanded the range of ideological and philosophical inquiry. But it fell short of raising the ideology to a qualitatively new, higher level. The values common to all humankind, when removed from the context of class, national, and geopolitical realities, proved to be socially and politically diluted and devoid of real content.

This failure can be seen most readily in international relations— usually claimed to be among the indisputable achievements of perestroika. The deideologization of international relations turned out to be unilateral. It gave all the advantages to the other side. The "new political thinking" at first obscured the ideological contradiction between labor and capital and then began to distract us from the basic great-power contradictions. The dialectical unity between ideological struggle and political cooperation was first deformed and then replaced by an imagined unity between the two essentially different systems of the West and the East.

This process had far-reaching consequences for our society. The creators of the ideology of renewal had surrendered to the values of the Western way of life. Their unrestrained propaganda in favor of this way of life replaced the myth of "developed socialism" with the myth of "developed capitalism."

Deideologization had a similar result inside our country: under the pretext of a renewed ideology, eclecticism and populism became the main positions.

Those philosophers and political thinkers who saw concepts such as "perestroika," "acceleration," "the human factor," "a qualitatively new social state," "socialist choice," and the formula "more democracy is more socialism" as illusions of theoretical novelty—a smokescreen to conceal retreat—were correct. All these concepts were devoid of any real content and could be interpreted—and indeed were—to suit the needs of a given person or group of people.

Since late 1991, the dynamics of our country's transition have changed from supporting reforms within the framework of formational changes to radical efforts to destroy the lifestyle and the accompanying way of thought that developed after the 1917 October Revolution.

The introduction of such drastic measures resulted in the disintegration of the USSR; the emergence of independent states; the liquidation of a unique type of state system, the system of soviets [councils] of all levels; a dismantling of the integrated national economic complex that had formed over decades; an unprecedented decline in production, accompanied by the collapse of entire previously successful branches of the economy; a steady decline in living standards for millions of people, accompanied by a decline in the birth rate and a rise in the mortality rate comparable to times of the fiercest wars; the disintegration of a unified society into a confused mass of people who are swiftly losing their traditional system of values and ideals; the appearance of a mafia-corrupted class; an unprecedented outburst of crime and corruption; and a threat to our once preeminent science and education, to our culture, and to our material and spiritual environment.

What actually has taken place in Russia during the past ten years? What were the real reasons for Russia's latest time of troubles? What are the main driving forces at work here? Who are the executors and the leaders? What are our real prospects? What must be done to gain control of the situation? How can we emerge from this political, economic, and ideological impasse? What price must be paid for the mythical "freedom," misplaced trust, general carelessness, and foolhardiness on the part of millions of Russians and the treachery, lust for power, scheming, and malice on the part of a few individuals?

We are faced with vital questions concerning Russia's new place and role in a new geopolitical situation. With the disappearance of a bipolar mechanism for regulating international affairs, determined predominantly by relations between the USSR and the United States, an entirely different global configuration of forces has emerged.

There are the United States, Western Europe (in which a united Germany is not quite accommodated), Russia (which in spite of its internal instability and weakness still cannot be written off as a great power), China with its more than one billion people, Japan, with India on the horizon and Brazil "looming" in the distance. The new configuration of forces will compel the Arab countries of the Middle East to unite to deal with these new uncertainties. Indeed, the new geopolitical equation has many unknowns. And this makes it much more difficult to balance all these various emerging interests.

Along with major changes in political, economic, and military inequalities on our planet, global problems of human civilization are becoming more complicated with each year. Today we face crises in raw-material and energy resources, radioactive and electromagnetic pollution, the destruction of the ozone layer, the deterioration of ecological conditions, the emergence and spread of new diseases, actual and potential regional and international conflicts, and increased individual and group violence at the community level.

It is no longer just Russia and the former republics of the USSR but the whole planet that must urgently choose and implement comprehensive philosophies of survival.

III

The uncertainty about Russia's role and place in the world community, especially after the signing of the agreements in the Belovezh Forest

Preserve in December 1991,[4] shows the importance of developing civilizational and geopolitical approaches. This problem attracted the special attention of our scholars during the 1960s and 1970s in connection with the emerging of the task of achieving military-strategic parity between the USSR and the United States, but it became particularly popular during perestroika. With some significant reservations, it was then accepted that socialism had its own role to play as a world system, both as a nucleus of the world revolutionary process and as a geopolitical structure expressing the characteristics of a civilization. By the same token, it was seen that our country had its own global interests, determined by its place and importance in the development of mankind.

The theoretical search for civilizational and geopolitical solutions was complicated by a number of attendant circumstances, such as, for example, the disregard of any phenomena that did not readily fit in with simplified and vulgarized interpretations of Marxist theories of socioeconomic formations, especially when evaluating changes in spiritual life and ethnic relations, and that during the period of perestroika hampered the efforts of "architects" and "foremen" to substantiate the new political thinking by casting doubts on these efforts. Similar errors can be seen now as well in the development of Russia's official foreign policy.

By overcoming these and similar complications, we can again come to understand Russia's historical experience as an amalgam of European and Asian civilizations, a phenomenon poorly understood in terms of its sociopolitical characteristics. A comprehensive understanding of the mechanisms of sociopolitical changes in modern Russian society is only now forming. The same is true of the philosophy of current politics in general. The main building blocks of this philosophy are the following:

• an affirmation of pluralism in cognitive methodology;
• a recognition of equality for various ideological-political theories and doctrines, except those that pursue antihuman goals;
• the priority of tolerance over confrontation in regard to different, even diametrically opposite, points of view;
• the acceptance strictly on the basis of scholarly and social merit of the most promising blueprints for social development, both atheistic and religious.

These components will enable us to outline ways for solving our main strategic task for the long-term survival of Russia—the acquisition of a constructive worldview and of spiritual health for our nation.

Our times demand that we create an effective and modern "ideology of patriotism." Such an ideology can be the firm philosophical basis for the functioning of the Russian state and can establish Russia as the powerful alternative center of worldwide influence capable of embodying justice, democracy, and the social, political, cultural, and economic principles of a "continental" direction of development for the future.

IV

When thinking about the future, it is always prudent to consult those who were thinking about the same problems before us.

When analyzing our theory of civilizations, we should remember the earlier studies of Nikolai Danilevsky and Konstantin Leontyev.[5] In his famous book *Russia and Europe*, Danilevsky analyzed the historical process from ancient times to his own days and, using his findings, criticized the main evolutionist principle of historical scholarship, which assumed a sequential, progressive development of mankind from lower to higher cultural forms.

"A natural system of history," Danilevsky wrote, "should accept for its division the principle of distinguishing among cultural-historical types." Danilevsky's "cultural-historical type" is his scholarly term for the historical phenomenon that today is becoming known in professional circles as "civilization."

To understand fully the spiritual foundations of the Russian state philosophy and Russian patriotism expressed by the collective concept "the Russian idea," without a modern interpretation of which our search for ways to restore the state-political body of our country within the historical parameters characteristic of it is hardly feasible, we should also refer to the writings of Vladimir Solovyov and Nikolai Berdyaev; the religious philosophers Sergei and Evgeny Trubetskoy, Pavel Florensky, and Sergei Bulgakov; and the historian of the Russian Orthodox Church Alexander Kartashev.[6]

The works of some foreign authors are of interest here as well, particularly the scholarly findings of Oswald Spengler. In *The Decline of the West*, he attempted to specify the West European–American situation between 1800 and 2000 in world historical terms. His conclusion was not encouraging: "We, the people of the Western European culture, of a period precisely delimited in time from the tenth to the twentieth centuries, are an exception rather than the rule. . . . And perhaps with the expiration of the civilization of the West, whose carriers we are now, culture and therefore the human type . . .will not appear again." And further: "The decline of the West, examined from this angle, represents neither more nor less than a problem of civilization. Here before us is one of the basic questions of history: What is civilization, comprehended as the logical consequence and as the end and outcome of any culture?"[7]

I believe we should give attentive consideration to the key postulates of Arnold Toynbee's theory of the historical development of humankind, as well as to Francis Fukuyama's concept of the "end of history."[8]

Lev Gumilyov, who died so prematurely, left us a theoretical legacy that is highly relevant to modern political and philosophical doctrines and to history as a whole. Because of the originality of his ideas, the scale of his scholarly discoveries, and his force of spiritual and moral greatness, Gumilyov should be seen as one of the most outstanding philosophers and systematicians of the twentieth century. Gumilyov's theory of "passionarity"[9] is a seminal contribution to the theory of ethnogenesis, the genesis of civilizations on the territories of Russia; it has also provided a powerful impetus to seek nontraditional methods and approaches to the analysis of the objective tendencies and real mechanisms of sociopolitical change, especially in dealing with periods critical for Russia's destiny.

V

Russian society cannot advance without a clear realization of the specific features of its historical path, the character of the problems it faces, and the principles and purposes that should form the basis of a promising model of development.

We need to understand the objective processes occurring in the world with regard to material production, science and technology, spirituality, and social, political, national, and ideological relations. We must have a good understanding of the condition and role of power structures in the life of modern society and the role of concentrated capital in the hands of national and transnational groups acting as the initiators, organizers, and directors of the power that capital represents. We must also trace the changing relations among countries during a time of increasing shortage of raw materials and energy and keen competition for consumer markets.

We must perform a complex philosophical and political analysis of the objective tendencies and mechanisms of the social changes in Russia during the past decade. We must propose a national-state doctrine that is based on an analysis of our long-term interests and the tendencies of our country's development, of the spirit and character of the people, and of the original laws governing our country's national, economic, and cultural development.

Experience, common sense, scientific analysis, and cultural tradition confirm that:

• from a historical point of view, Russia is a unique civilization, having inherited and passing on the thousand-year-old traditions of Kievan Rus, Muscovy, the Russian Empire, and the USSR;

• geopolitically, Russia is the core and the mainstay of the Eurasian continental bloc, whose interests oppose the hegemonic tendencies of the "oceanic power" of the United States and the Atlantic "great space";

• in ideology and worldview, Russia represents the cultural-historical and moral traditions and fundamental values of communality, collectivism, great-power sovereignty (state self-sufficiency), and the aspiration to embody the highest ideals of good and justice;

• in national terms, Russia is a complex ethnic community resting on a powerful national nucleus of Russians, Ukrainians, and Belarusians;

• from an economic point of view, Russia is an autonomous economic mechanism that differs distinctly in the rules by which it operates from the Western "free market model."

The author agrees with those scholars who believe that the uniqueness of Russia's development stems directly from all the elements of its character: its mode of production, its social life, its population or human potential, its mode of material production, and its geographic environment. This uniqueness was formed by the way in which the contradictions between society and nature were manifested in the given region. These contradictions have shaped the specific features of

Russia's internal situation and the "special soul" of the Russian people.

The coming period of Russia's development should be considered as a period of stabilization. During this period, it is above all necessary to minimize the damage inflicted recently upon our country by the unreasoned actions of politicians. It is essential to work out mechanisms to mobilize all potential resources in society for leading the country out of its deep systemic crisis. We must ensure that priority is given to internal problems of social renewal and national revival, while keeping state involvement in external affairs to a minimum.

Similar situations have arisen more than once during Russia's thousand-year history, and each time our ancestors were able to overcome them with honor. Let us recall the gathering one by one around Moscow of small principalities ruined by Tatar-Mongol and Teutonic invasions; the employment of assemblies of the land to overcome the Time of Troubles in the sixteenth and seventeenth centuries; the forced opening of a "window to Europe" by Peter the Great; Chancellor Gorchakov's famous motto "Russia is concentrating," after the failures of the Crimean War and the unjustified delay in the emancipation of the serfs;[10] the restoration of our country's state unity and economic might after the fall of tsarism and the Provisional Government in 1917; and, finally, the swift revival of our country and its advancement to a leading position in the world after our victory in the Great Patriotic War of 1941–45.

VI

The analysis of the geopolitical situation in the second half of the nineteenth century and the first half of the twentieth that is based on the methodology of Karl Marx and Vladimir Lenin, who took class antagonism as a starting point, has proven to be completely valid. This is why this methodology, partially or completely (sometimes without mention of its authorship), has been used as a component in practically all realistic thinking about global politics. The class-antagonism approach remains valid today in addressing many key problems, especially in production, employment, social security, foreign-policy guidelines, and international relations.

But the realities of the end of the twentieth century, and of the approaching twenty-first century, will be more difficult, more complex, and far more variable than the conditions facing Marx and Lenin.

Today, not only relations between classes but also relations between civilizations lie at the heart of the dynamic and development mechanisms of sociopolitical change.

Indeed, intercivilizational and intracivilizational relations, with their attendant contradictions, are absorbing class contradictions. And, while not removing them completely, at certain stages these dynamic contradictions are at least partly able to level or reduce the confrontational components of interclass relations. World War II was not only a war fought by two social class systems, it was also a war determined by a principle that is central to scientific geopolitics: "people—territory—lifestyle."

German fascism intended to destroy the USSR not only as the homeland of socialism but more urgently as the nucleus of a new geopolitical structure. This fact brought about the anti-Hitler coalition that included disparate states with different political systems and ideologies.

In today's Russia and over the entire space of the former USSR, the main conflict is not among the basic classes and social strata but among the ruling regimes based on a thin stratum of either a compradorian or a nationalistic "mafia," which in pursuit of its selfish aims is aspiring to destroy the Eurasian civilization represented by Russia. It is a conflict between the unifying tendencies of Russia's natural development and the entirely subjective volitional tendencies of the narrowly corporate group that has seized power in the post-Soviet republics.

The Breakdown

The imperative to change every facet of life in Russian (Soviet) society and to formulate a new strategy has taken shape over a long period of time. Inside our country, the state form of ownership, which has swallowed the collective form of ownership, has in essence become a monopoly in the whole vast USSR, effectively liquidating any basis for competition and competitiveness and turning them into mere formalities. As a consequence, the natural, objective source of progress within the social system has disappeared.

The CPSU became a subjective factor in the development of socialist society. The resolutions of the CPSU Central Committee and the decisions of its plenary sessions were used as incentives for the fulfillment of plans for industry, agriculture, culture, education, and all other national activities. Various forms of administrative pressure were also used in this process.

Arbitrary decision making in management resulted in the unequal development of various branches of the national economy. The preponderance of attention given by the Party to the development of heavy industry stifled the development of light industry and the food industry and, naturally, affected the living standard of the people.

Command methods used in agriculture depressed the initiative of rural workers, leading to a decline in labor productivity, especially in such labor-intensive areas as animal husbandry.

Without access to financial resources, industrial enterprises could not update their equipment, introduce new technologies, or take advantage of the most recent achievements in science and engineering. The scientific establishment itself, except for the defense branches, lost the stimulus for development that should have been provided by demand for new projects and technical innovations.

Rigid centralization of the management of society had its advantages in the initial stages of socialist construction, during the Great Patriotic War, and during the postwar restoration of the economy. But by the end of the 1960s, it had totally exhausted itself. Problems began to spring up faster than they could be solved, resulting in more (and more distinctly visible) stagnation: a sharp decline in the rate of economic growth (from 7–8 percent in the early 1970s to 1–2 percent by the beginning of the 1980s); a slow paralysis of the administrative centers; a reduction in the growth of the well-being of the population; and the accumulation and spread of other related negative phenomena.

At the beginning of the 1980s, the following contradictions of social development were clearly discernible: between the monopoly of state ownership and the centralized system of management based on it, and the growing need for self-management by large industrial and agricultural enterprises, scientific centers, and highly developed regions of the country; between the intensive development of group "A" enterprises, especially those of the military complex, and group "B" enterprises;[11] between a high degree of industrial development, and the backwardness of agriculture; between ossified production relations, and an increasing production potential; between the growth of the volume of goods produced, and a decline in consumption by the population because of the limited selection of consumer goods; between the tendency to unify culture, and the aspiration to keep and develop ethnic cultures; and between the official policy of atheism, and the reality of the people's religiosity.

A sociopsychological breakdown occurred, which manifested itself in the indifference of the general population to changes in political power in our country and to the eventual removal of the CPSU from the levers of power.

Outside our country, the military-strategic parity that had developed between the USSR and the United States promoted a shift away from the "cold war" and toward a lessening of international tensions. However, this shift, which was imposed by circumstances and was limited to strategic arms, did nothing to eliminate the political and economic contradictions with the West. Certain contradictions growing within the commonwealth of socialist countries mirrored the situation in the USSR, and the West lost no time in exploiting what it perceived to be opportunities to foster distrust and foment dissension.

Finally, it is necessary to note the third group of contradictions— those within the Western world: between highly developed countries and underdeveloped countries, and also among the highly developed countries themselves for control of consumer markets, energy, and natural resources. We can conclude that the rivalry between the United States and the USSR stemmed not so much from differences of ideology as from competition for political and economic influence in the world.

Those researchers are correct who look at these processes through a prism of changes occurring in our country and in the context of relations within the entire civilized world. The main tendency of these changes is clear, although they developed differently in various regions and are proceeding with political, socioeconomic, ideological, spiritual, and other consequences of unequal severity and intensity. This is above all a process of adapting socioeconomic systems to the changing needs of the scientific-technical revolution, accompanied by a striving to establish a uniform structure of cumulative productive forces that can serve as a basis for new social formations.

The reforms of Mikhail Gorbachev began in the wake of a global tendency to transform socioeconomic systems. The powerful restraints of centralism that had repressed people's creative freedom began to ease gradually. The welfare, social security, and freedom of the people began to be regarded as paramount values. Discussions about personal responsibility, individual uniqueness, and the harmonious development of the personality gained momentum.

The balance between common and private interests began to shift in favor of easing the domination of common interests over private ones. Constrained for so long, the human desire for self-expression manifested itself in various forms, including some nonstandard ones. Society began to realize that radical transformations were in order. Some of the specific measures that were considered were the introduction of new technical achievements to compensate for flagging labor energy and declining enthusiasm; the creation of economic levers for creative work; improvements in agriculture; a radical improvement in the quality of services and medical care; a reform of the system of education, physical fitness, and sports; a democratization of the political system; and a raising of culture and of the provision of cultural services to the population to a qualitatively new level.

It would be wrong to say that the country's leadership failed to perceive the need for change. More and more each year, officials at all levels were becoming aware that a mechanism had to be found that was capable of giving due dynamism to socioeconomic development. As a result, a model for reorganization took shape that was designed to embrace all socioeconomic changes, at first within the framework of the existing political and social system and later on a much broader scale.

However, as we know from historical experience, common sense, and scientific analysis, no reform can be implemented successfully without a well-developed program and precisely defined goals; a team of vigorous and highly intellectual reformers; a strong and effective system for controlling political phenomena; thoroughly developed and carefully considered methods of instituting the reforms; the mobilization of the mass media to explain the meaning, goals, and consequences of the reforms for the state as a whole and for the individual person in particular for the purpose of involving as much of the population as possible in the reform process; and the preservation and development of the structures, relations, functions, methods, and lifestyles that have earned the approval of the people.

The reform process in China (PRC) developed along approximately similar lines. But nothing like this was done by Mikhail Gorbachev and his team. Labor collectives, party organizations, economic leaders, and much of the intelligentsia were excluded from participating in the renewal of society. The right to define directions and interpret the meaning of the reorganization processes was appropriated by a small group of top leaders, who were given to superficial improvisation and were unable to organize and direct the reform properly. They were backed by "national fronts," national-egoists, elite groups, and various informal associations. Instead of the hard work that was urgently needed, they unfolded a parade of political arrogance, demagoguery, and dilettantism, which gradually overwhelmed and paralyzed the country.

Under the guise of a struggle against the former system, the uniform structures of public and state management and control were targeted for elimination. But in eliminating the obsolete administrative-command system, the new "reformers" simultaneously destroyed the basic structural elements of legitimate power necessary in any state. As a result, economic ties were seriously damaged and labor, technological, contractual, and state discipline were seriously undermined. The virus of private profiteering was allowed to penetrate the very organism of the national economy.

Society now found itself in a state of deep crisis, fueled by public charges against the old system: the statization of all aspects of social life; the dictatorial rule of Party chiefs; officially sanctioned arbitrariness and lawlessness; destructive misuse of natural resources; dogmatism and intolerance toward different opinions; and mindless belligerence in foreign policy.

The crisis was exacerbated by major errors and miscalculations in implementing the key goals and purposes of perestroika. The economy collapsed and descended into general chaos; attempts to end egalitarian "leveling" resulted in complete disregard for social justice. And most of Russia's people rapidly became poorer.

Domestic policy suffered from a disregard for the growing tensions in society and antagonistic political disagreements; a misunderstanding, and sometimes encouragement, of separatist moods in the union republics; the growth of nationalism and anti-Russian feeling in non-Russian areas; the unfolding of a struggle for power at the very top that caused many to question its legitimacy; loss of public trust in the ability of the leadership to restore order and deal with urgent daily problems; and the precipitous decline of society into a "cold" civil war.

Foreign policy produced, with some improvements on the international scene, a breakdown of the strategic parity between East and

West, which had been achieved by the extreme efforts of several generations of the Soviet people. For the first time in many decades, our country was without real military-political allies.

Some farsighted political leaders both in the West and in the East wanted to deal with the USSR as a reliable, stable, and peaceful partner, not as a hungry country plagued by social and ethnic conflict, and even less did they want to deal with a dozen mutually antagonistic dwarf states equipped with modern arms, saber-rattling over disputed borders.

But in addition to these kinds of politicians, there were (and still are) transnational companies that look upon the Soviet Union as a potential source of raw materials to be exploited with the help of our (rather cheap) labor. Well-financed special services of various countries continue to work against us. Our domestic mafia structures have long maintained ties with international criminal organizations, especially with profascist groups and drug lords. But this is less disturbing than the fact that rogues both here and abroad are all too often able to find high-ranking patrons in the government and state structures of our country.

The following conclusion is unavoidable. A deep modernization of our country was necessary long before the coming of perestroika. Our society had outgrown the narrow framework of the Brezhnev type of socialism, and our economy had outgrown the primitive logic of bureaucratic planning. It was tragic for the USSR that the Party nomenklatura had long ago rejected the idea of careful but rapid reform, a reform that eschewed the demolition of the historical traditions of Russian civilization. But now a vulgarized form of Marxism has been replaced by a vulgarized form of Eurocentrism, according to which every country should imitate the West. Within the framework of this Eurocentrism, Russia adopted the social philosophy of neoliberalism, which was experiencing a temporary surge at that time.

This philosophy became the basis for the reforms. Instead of a smooth transition to such social-democratic models as Sweden or West Germany, as was proposed by the ideologist of the democrats Andrei Sakharov,[12] a "great leap" to the American prototype took place. This revolution brought us ruin and suffering. It wrenched our country away from the mixed, socially oriented economy that we could have gradually achieved by starting from the prevailing conditions of 1989. Revolution, especially when it involves violence, leaves us two bleak alternatives: paternalism, even in the form of war communism,[13] or the extinction of the population. Today we are being pushed toward the latter.

By the middle of 1991, the political map of Moscow had assumed a curious and distinctive form. On the surface, the old Party nomenklatura continued to hold the important levers of power. They completely controlled the power structures. The party-state vertical, although already quite battered and shaken during the six years of perestroika and therefore not as reliable as it had been earlier, remained an experienced professional instrument in matters of the administrative and economic management of personnel. The national legislative body—the Supreme Soviet of the USSR—could in cases of necessity muster a majority vote to pass stabilization measures, albeit not as easily and painlessly as before. The central television station and most of the regional stations, as well as a significant part of the central and local press, remained in the hands of the Party. The mass media were capable of carrying on their functions when ordered to do so by those at the top.

The Party had, if not all, then almost all the resources it needed to manage the economy and society as a whole. However, the most important thing was already missing: the central organism of the Party entirely lacked effective and purposeful political will. The attempt to fill this gap by reconstructing the Communist Party of the RSFSR did not produce the expected effect. There was not enough time. The activity of the Communist Party of the RSFSR began under extremely complicated conditions. With the blessing of the Politburo of the Central Committee of the CPSU, virtually all the mass media launched a concentrated attack on the new branch party and worked to discredit its leadership.

As a result, the tired and aged CPSU, which was slated for sacrifice by its own leaders, had not the strength to act on its instinct of self-preservation and adopt essential security and self-defense measures. Nevertheless, by continuing by force of habit, and often as a mere formality, to control the heights of political power, the CPSU appeared to present an insuperable obstacle on the path of the new political forces striving to take its place. Moreover, there was still some "danger" (small but real) that some healthy reforms inside the Party could ignite a spark of new life in its huge body.

As a result, the "democratic" elite had to ensure an abrupt and instantaneous "dumping" of its opponents and destroy the CPSU's mechanisms of political domination.

This quasi-democratic elite, formed during the years of perestroika, consisted of party renegades, bureaucratic opportunists sensitive to the slightest changes in the political climate, "agents of influence," dissidents, defenders of human rights, a part of the denationalized "creative" intelligentsia, and other splinter groups. Unshaped and motley, they would have had no chance of victory were it not for the fully developed objective reasons described earlier and a number of subjective factors that proved to be decisive in this situation.

First, only their maniacal will to attain power united this amorphous, assorted crowd into a cohesive team. We are talking here only about those who worked consciously, not about the huge majority of well-meaning people who were charmed by the new slogans and populist appeals.

Second, after decades of dull, tired slogans and ideological stagnation, the liberal-democratic ideology looked attractive. The unsophisticated Russian public found it almost impossible to discern the hypocrisy of the clamorous promoters of this ideology behind its bright-colored facade. This was an ideology that ensured for the democrats the unconditional support of the West, with all its accompanying material and organizational benefits. But this ideology also concealed a destructive seed, the first shoots of which coincided with the disintegration of the USSR and the first fruits of which were seen at the time of the October tragedy in Moscow.[14]

Third, and most importantly, the democrats had some influential allies in their opponent's camp. The "monolithic unity" of the CPSU turned out to be hollow, and a significant part of the nomenklatura, attracted by promises "to live as they do in Switzerland," formed a "fifth column" within the Party ready at any moment to sell themselves to the highest bidder. Paradoxically, at the head of this army of traitors and deserters was the general secretary of the Central Committee of the CPSU [Mikhail Gorbachev] with his closest supporters.

Yet another force, a regional one, appeared in the political arena. It consisted of the political elites of the union republics of the USSR. In most cases their political wisdom alas amounted to no more than a desire to seize as much power and wealth as possible and to grab as many rights and privileges as they could. In their pursuit of these longings, they were ever ready to support the highest bidder.

All this clearly doomed the Party. The only question was whether the change in authority would come through evolutionary or revolutionary means. The former would have allowed the continuation of a uniform state and a healthy reform of society; the latter brought the collapse of our country, a dangerous weakening of Russia, and, as a consequence, a powerful geopolitical shift in favor of the West.

Controlled Catastrophe

A major indicator of sociopolitical change in the beginning of the 1990s was the heightening of social conflict. The failure of perestroika as a mechanism for resolving an agonistic but reconcilable conflict led first to a chronic and then rapidly to an antagonistic conflict that affected not only individuals and pressure groups but all social strata and political groupings. The content of the conflict was defined by a struggle for and retention of power.

From the moment when the political grouping of the radical "Westernizers" managed—with the support of the world oligarchy and at the price of the disintegration of the USSR—to assume political power in Russia, it was clear that the Russian people would not accept the type of development that was being imposed on them. It was also obvious that the number of those who were dissatisfied would grow as poverty increased and the general chaos spread—both inevitable consequences of the political and economic course of the new Russian leadership. Eventually that discontent would reach a critical point and then endanger the laborious efforts of the powerful international forces committed to removing Russia from the geopolitical arena by every means possible.

But to keep such a huge country in check without resorting to force is practically impossible. So the plan had to be more realistic: to develop and implement a technique for the controlled transformation of the country to a new political mode with dictatorial elements. This scenario envisions establishing secret, complete, and rigid international control over the political situation in Russia, ensuring that the national-patriotic forces in Russia are kept away from the levers of state power.

By analyzing the political and social collisions in Russia, we can solve many riddles of recent history. The tragicomic coup of August 1991 can be viewed in a new light. [16] The striking parallels between the positions of the "putschists" in August 1991 and the "rebels" in October 1993 become clear. From this vantage point, it is even possible to forecast with some accuracy the political situation in the near future.

The technique used can be conditionally labeled a technique of "controlled explosions" or a "controlled catastrophe." Its main purpose is the systematic elimination from the Russian political arena of all forces that could hinder the integration of the country into the united supragovernmental system of the "new world order." This approach exploits the political and social antagonisms that naturally exist in any country, and especially in countries like Russia, in periods of deep systemic crisis. The starting point for the use of this technique is determined by political reality. The final goal is the transformation of the entire sociopolitical system into a new entity with precisely programmed characteristics.

To outline this process, let us assume the presence of the following participants: the "players," who are pursuing independent political goals: and the "conductor," whose goal is to ensure everybody's adherence to certain rules of the game guaranteeing the desired result. In fact, the "conductor" is also a "player," but of a higher order. He plays and simultaneously pursues his own goal, which is concealed from the majority of the "players."

The whole process can be divided into five consecutive phases.

The first phase is the setting. This entails a determination by the "conductor" of his attitude toward the "players." The "players" are divided into allies and opponents. The main criterion ensuring a sufficient degree of accuracy for this division is the attitude of the "players" toward certain fundamental, standard concepts and requirements that reflect the true goals of the "conductor" in this game. By finding out what those "standards" are in all areas of life, we can identify the actual, rather than the illusory, driving forces of the "game."

Assuming that an external force interested in the elimination of a strong rival is trying to be the "conductor" in the current Russian turmoil—as has happened so many times in our turbulent thousand-year-long history—we would have the following situation on the eve of the August 1991 coup:

1. The "conductor's" "standard" for choosing friends was the readiness of "players" to sacrifice the geopolitical interests of the USSR (Russia) in order to attain their individual political and material goals (power, wealth, etc.).

2. In the confrontation between "democrats" and "communists," the

natural allies of the "conductor" were the denationalized democrats, who professed their striving for "integration into the world economic system," for "inclusion in the market," for "the primacy of universal human values," and other such ideological bromides.

The second phase is cumulative and, ultimately, polarizing. The friends and enemies have been determined, and now they must be polarized to exclude any chance for a compromise between them. Around one pole, the "conductor" concentrates all those he intends to use to seize power after the game is over; around the other pole, he gathers those who must be removed from the political arena.

At this point, the question of personality becomes especially important. Russians do not accept faceless ideas. For an idea to have a chance to be implemented, it must be personalized. Given our conditions, it is difficult to overestimate the role of the individual, the personality, the colorful and energetic leader. That is why an experienced "conductor" tries to identify all the "players" of the opposite side, all the political leaders of the opposition, as belonging to one political group. The opposite pole, which is subject to elimination, should be given enough time to attract all the forces that are earmarked for "scrapping" and all the leaders whose elimination will guarantee that the friendly "players" allied with the "conductor" will have maximum freedom of action.

Applying this analysis to the era of perestroika, we will find that the period 1985–89 coincided with the first phase of the game and the period 1989–90 with the second phase.

The third phase is the crisis phase and is crucial for the game to succeed. Its implementation requires that the "conductor" be especially careful and thorough and that he be a sophisticated and skillful master of political intrigue. The task is to set opponents against each other and to fan subjective contradictions so as to exclude any chance of agreements aimed at resolving the crisis. Everything must be done to provoke clashes between "players" under conditions that are in advance adverse for the opponents of the "conductor" and favorable for his allies.

Events at the end of 1990 and the first half of 1991 in Russia developed according to this scenario. The collapse of the world socialist system, the progressive disintegration of the USSR, the rise of aggressive nationalism in the provinces, clashes in Lithuania, the inexplicable inactivity of the all-powerful general secretary and president, growing restlessness in the lower echelons of the Party, hysteria in the "democratic" mass media, the smear campaign against the army, the loss of all strategic allies, and the disregard for the March referendum,[15] which confirmed the unity of the country—all this resulted in a situation in which the Party, or, to be more precise, the Party's conservative-state wing, was now left with no choice: either it had to capitulate unconditionally in the face of these new realities, or else it had to undertake energetic actions aimed at stabilizing the USSR's internal and external position.

This is how the August "putsch" was provoked.

The fourth phase of the process calls for the use of force, or revolution. It takes the least time and is the most decisive. Its success depends almost completely on the thoroughness with which preparations were made in the preceding phase of the game. Certainly, some risks remain. However, given a competent "conductor," the risk is small.

This phase calls for the "players" to step outside the legal arena and away from political stereotypes. The resulting explosion creates ideal preliminary conditions for a decisive change in the political landscape. Being in shock, public opinion allows the winning "players" to conduct any revolutionary manipulations without fear of being held responsible or facing organized counteraction.

In the August coup, the unfortunate result for its organizers and participants was predetermined from the start. The following three factors doomed the attempt in advance:

1. The predictability of the event itself. The coup had been rumored to be in the making long before it was attempted. Thus, the main "players" knew that something like this was coming, and the most trusted among them had every opportunity to prepare themselves.

2. The carnival-like, timid, and indecisive quality of the event. Even the organizers themselves never made any serious plans. It was tacitly assumed that a show of determination and power would be sufficient to restore order and create a climate conducive to the implementation of stabilizing measures.

3. The bizarre (to put it mildly) behavior of the top leader of the Party and the state. The duplicity of the president and general secretary at this stage is obvious. His inactivity gave a "green light" to the organizers of the coup, but as soon as the situation became irreversible, he immediately denounced them. His personal political goals are plain and clear: to get rid of the constraining guardianship of the

"conservatives" and untie his hands for further political maneuvers.

The goals of the "conductor," however, were quite different, and the they are what predetermined the content of the fifth and final phase of the game.

The fifth phase can be defined as the phase of general collapse. As a result of the provoked political explosion, the hostile-power pole finds itself "outside the law" and is liquidated ruthlessly. The breakdown of the legal fabric and the paralysis of the stunned opponents allow the victorious "players" to crush any remaining opposition quickly, to take over all the commanding heights, and to change the situation to their own advantage, which is just what was envisioned by the technique according to which the "conductor" had acted.

In the case of the August coup, this final phase lasted until December 1991, at which time, as a result of the Belovezh deal, the USSR, the historical and geopolitical successor to the Russian Empire, was legally liquidated. The "perestroika era" ended, ushering in a new balance of power both within Russia and globally.

In brief, this technique can be expressed as follows: "SCHISM—CONFLICT—IMPASSE—EXPLOSION—COLLAPSE." The seed of schism is implanted in the ruling political grouping or the growth of an already existing schism is encouraged. Competing fractions are artificially polarized according to an either–or ideological choice: democracy or communism, cosmopolitanism or nationalism, capitalism or socialism, market or plan, and so forth. Contradictions are purposefully heated up, turning disputes into conflicts. Political impasse follows, and then severe crisis, during which the "hostile" political grouping is liquidated. If need be, everything can be repeated to deal with "undesirable" tendencies that may threaten to splinter the winning team. Repeated explosions of this type can serve to "filter" the political spectrum of the ruling elite, gradually removing unwelcome elements from all the structures of power and state management, destroying their social base, and effectively preventing their ideological and practical consolidation.

The Evolution of the Current Regime

The political construct that emerged in our country as a result of the state revolution in September and October and the elections of December 12, 1993, is extremely volatile. It must be stated above all that this construct represents the rule of a minority over a huge majority of the working people. This fact is admitted—even openly emphasized. Many officials make no secret of their goal to create a new class of proprietors, a new bourgeoisie, whose interests they intend to represent and protect.

A handful of people who grew rich by plundering public property are strengthening their dominant position in Russia. Because this looting occurred with the encouragement of the state power, this power itself is becoming criminalized, closely tying our bureaucrats with the criminal world and making corruption an accepted daily fact of life. The fact that the policies and actions of Russia's current leadership are encouraged by foreign capital means that we are ruled by a compradorian, antinational regime.

The purpose of the September–October government coup was to make state institutions conform to their new class identity. The destruction of the system of soviets [councils] transformed all representative bodies, both in the center and at the local level, into impotent appendages of the executive branch. The sharp limitation of parliamentary powers was accompanied by the virtual disappearance of those who represented the vast majority of the population—the workers and peasants. In their seats in national parliaments and local legislatures we now see bureaucrats.

As a consequence, control over the system of administration by elective representatives is being eroded. Ties between central and local representative bodies are being destroyed. We are witnessing the emergence of a dictatorial regime resting on a huge army of bureaucrats that is twice as large as it was three years ago.

The unchecked expansion of the president's administration has destroyed the principle of the division of powers enunciated in the new Constitution of Russia.

The Agreement on Public Consent, which was signed in April 1994 by a number of state and political structures, has hardly changed the basic characteristics of the regime. Today there is no branch of power in the whole state whose legitimacy could not be reasonably or justifiably challenged.

The president, who swore to uphold the Constitution, himself ignored its letter and spirit. The Federal Assembly was formed as a result of elections that circumvented the Constitution and were conducted undemocratically. The independence of the Constitutional Court is a hollow sham after the Court was blackmailed into silence.

Today, the "triangle," well known from prerevolutionary Russian parliamentary history, is back: an autocrat (tsar, president) not under the control of and not accountable to the people's government; a government appointed by the autocrat and also not under the control of the people; and, finally, a two-house parliament (under the tsar, the Duma and the State Council; now, the Duma and the Federation Council), in which the lower house has limited legislative (in fact, mere advisory) and budgetary powers and is totally deprived of control and supervisory functions. The autocrat can dismiss the parliament, but the parliament cannot influence the autocrat or the government.

During the economic and political crisis on the eve of the February revolution [in 1917], this system proved to be incapable of maintaining control of the situation. Attempts by the Duma majority (the so-called Progressive Bloc, the recent analogue of which was Russian Unity) to persuade the tsar to defy his court clique, led by Grigory Rasputin,[17] and entrust the formation of the government to the Duma failed.

As we know, we do not learn from history. The same archaic system was reintroduced in Russia after the establishment of the presidency, and it immediately produced the imbalances and contradictions of 1917. Now it is being reproduced in a more rigid, incorrigible form. Just as before, all contradictions center around the question of the parliament's actual power, the right of its majority to form and to control the government, and its ability to influence political and economic policies.

Russia will face complex problems in the future. These should not be underestimated. And yet there is hope. No antidemocratic measures can permanently arrest the public consciousness, and they cannot prevent the approaching changes.

Civil Peace

First, the term civil peace does not imply general fraternization and the elimination of all contradictions. It is the necessary social context for resolving differences without resorting to force. Struggle among various social tendencies is inevitable, but this need not lead to the destruction of the state, its economy, and its social and spiritual values. To avoid this, an inclusive social and political coalition based on the recognition of national interests and values should be formed. Such a movement should be able to neutralize politically, economically, and morally the "party of civil war," which represents criminal-compradorian, corrupt, and antisocial elements.

Given some good will and an elementary sense of social responsibility, the political spectrum of such a coalition can readily encompass communists, socialists, national-patriots, centrists, and state-oriented democrats.

Second, movement toward the reestablishment of civil peace cannot be reduced to verbal obeisances but must be supported by concrete steps. The action steps and conditions necessary for a national reconciliation include:

• changing the socioeconomic course and developing a national-state doctrine that takes into account the thousand-year experience of Russian statehood; it is clear that Russia cannot overcome the crisis outside a socialist framework of development;

• forming a government of national trust that works with the parliamentary majority and is under the control of the State Duma;

• ending the humiliation of the army, the state security forces, and the militia and guaranteeing that they will not be used as a gendarmerie or as instruments of political struggle;

• abstaining from ideological revenge and from contempt for science, culture, and the traditional religions;

• immediately repaying what is owed to peasants, reestablishing the salaries of workers and employees, granting medical care and support to the elderly, restoring opportunities of free education to children and to college students;

• taking emergency measures against corruption, organized crime, and banditry;

• guaranteeing an objective presentation of the positions of all political forces by the state mass media, and preserving nationwide information channels; and

• restoring a renewed and voluntary multinational union on the initiative of the Russian Federation.

Civil peace is not created by the single act of a signed declaration. And our desire to promote its realization should determine our attitude toward all sociopolitical realities: the president and his administration; the government; draft laws and public initiatives; political parties; and strikes and other mass displays of protest.

As shown by the course of event at the end of 1994 and in early 1995, the situation in our country can change as abruptly as it did in August 1991.

The present political regime in Russia has lost the support not only of the poorest part of the population but also of those social strata on which it leaned in the beginning of its term—the large-scale and petty bourgeoisie, a part of the creative and scientific intelligentsia, and private farmers.

The Chechen crisis irreversibly compromised the regime. Even the democrats, who without hesitation supported the destruction of the White House in October 1993, in January 1995 were talking about the emergence of a new dictatorship. The peasantry, which is being pushed deeper and deeper into ruin, is coming out more and more actively against the regime. The working class, which is faced with poverty, unemployment, and a real threat of disqualification and starvation, is beginning to wake up. The intelligentsia, too, is beginning to see through all the "charms" of the government's destructive policy.

In our country, especially in its complex political and economic situation, it is not easy to predict the near future. However, both the logic of unfolding events and the objective tendencies of self-preservation make it possible to say that "democracy" in its present form will inevitably be replaced with a socioeconomic and political system that is more in harmony with the national spirit of the people.

The Russian State System

In investigating the reasons for the present crisis of the Russian state system, we should not limit our search to the responsibility of the political forces that ruled our country during previous decades. We should also look at the meaning of Russian statehood, which has been discussed so extensively and thoroughly by many of our outstanding thinkers.

The emergence of a stable Russian state system is tied to a spiritual phenomenon—the conversion of Russia to Christianity in 988. The adoption of Christianity united numerous freedom-loving Slavic tribes —Polane, Drevliane, Krivichi, Viatichi, Radimichi, and others—and initiated the formation of the unique ethnopolitical society that is known to the world as the "Russian people." Since that time, every important period of our history has coincided with stages of the spiritual development of Russia.

The foundations of Russian statehood have always been and still remain a great-power thinking, formational diversity, nationality, spirituality, and patriotism, all of which is contained in the collective concept of the "Russian idea," eventually becoming the nucleus of another concept—the "all-Russian idea."

In its classical form, the "Russian idea" does not recognize state power as being self-sufficient but defines its main purpose rather as the creation of optimal conditions for the achievement of justice and of personal, family, and social moral ideals. The entire ideology of a "symphony of powers"—spiritual, moral-religious, state, and secular —is based on this credo.

Every time this "symphonic" principle was violated, the internal rifts in our society became deeper and more difficult to mend. At such times, the spiritual condition of society ceased to be the top-priority care of the state. The inevitable consequence of a discrepancy between the external greatness of our country and the fragmented or disturbed internal ideological condition of society has been a crisis in national self-awareness resulting in the disintegration of the state system.

From the moment the uniform and centralized Muscovite state was founded in the tenth century as the legitimate successor of the ancient Kievan Rus, Russian statehood ascended "from strength to strength" as an imperial state system. Following the catastrophe of 1914–17, which revealed the complete failure of the exhausted old ruling classes, our country regained its bearings through a rebirth of great-power principles resting on a new social foundation.

Russia has long perceived itself as the successor and keeper of the great-power imperial legacy. This was powerfully expressed in the designation "Moscow as the Third Rome" coined by the monk Filofei at the end of the fifteenth century and the beginning of the sixteenth.

According to more recent interpretations, the historical relay from Rome through Byzantium to Moscow resulted in the formation of the three central postulates of imperial statehood: the Roman legal and commanding unity was enriched by Byzantine spiritual and moral Christian unity and finally culminated in the national unity of Muscovite Rus—Russia. This was later articulated by the formula "Autocracy, Orthodoxy, Nationality," which was advanced some 150 years ago by the Russian minister of education Sergei Uvarov.[18]

The revolution of 1917 was a natural result of the crisis that affected all aspects of state life and national self-awareness. From the moment of its emergence, the new state—the USSR—had to struggle with serious contradictions. On the one hand, the huge historical inertia of the Russian state system and its great-power tradition of national self-awareness steadily pushed the Soviet Union to accept the geopolitical role that Russia had historically played. On the other hand, the sharp break with thousand-year-long state and spiritual traditions, the categorical denial of historical continuity, a wholesale disparagement of old ideals, and a persistent nihilism in relation to national values had an extremely negative effect on our country's development.

The situation changed significantly with the beginning of the Great Patriotic War. An appeal to patriotism and to the historical traditions of Russia provided the drive for our victory over Germany. The unprecedently rapid reconstruction of our war-devastated economy was based on a conscious shift in domestic policy toward the recognition of national values and the rejection of dogmatic utopian myths, official Russophobia, and the shameless antichurch campaign.

The "Khrushchev thaw," which came a few years later, can be called a rehearsal for Gorbachev's perestroika. As now, "conductors" then cynically used people's trust and longing for justice. To the accompaniment of speeches urging the rehabilitation of the victims of political repressions (which was indeed urgently needed), the spiritual heirs of all those who hate Russia managed to curtail and freeze the early signs of a national Russian revival.

The period of Khrushchev's leadership and the years of "stagnation" that followed were skillfully used by these activists to restore and strengthen their positions in all segments of the administrative-informational structures. But at the grassroots level of the Party and among a significant part of its leading staff, state-oriented patriotic convictions continued to be strengthened and to mature, along with an understanding of the fact that we would have no future without the buttress of our great, thousand-year-old legacy.

By the middle of the 1980s, it became clear that the inevitable "change of generations" would usher in political leaders of the new type, who valued the national great-power ideals that history had bequeathed them. Terrified by this prospect, our external and internal enemies activated every variation of the "personnel game"—appointments, transfers, promotions, and demotions.

The main conclusions that can be drawn from the bitter experience of the collapse of our Soviet and the serious crisis of our Russian federal state system are the following:

• we must restore democracy, that is, the power of the vast majority of the working population;

• the economic footing during the period of the restoration of our state system should be a mixed economy, retaining the leading role of national ownership and state regulation of production, and also retaining and strengthening all the basic socioeconomic rights of working people;

• only constitutional federalism can be the principle underlying the construction of a multinational Russian state;

• the cornerstone of Russian state policy must be the comprehensive and free development of the ethnic uniqueness of the nations that have ties their historical fates with Russia.

For an Independent Foreign Policy

A comprehensive understanding of the processes that determine world politics is the essential prerequisite of an effective foreign-policy doctrine for Russia. In our view, today's state of international relations has been determined by the following factors:

• an increase in global crisis phenomena in all areas of human activity—from economics and politics to culture and religion;

• a collapse of geopolitical equilibrium, which had been guaranteed for the past three centuries by Russia (the USSR);

• the start of the implementation of plans to establish a "new world order" envisioning the introduction of a global regime of political, economic, and military dictatorship by the West, led by the United States.

The model of development of the "rich" Western countries, populated by the "golden billion" of oversupplied consumers, is unacceptable and impossible for the other, much larger part of humankind. Any attempt to repeat it would accelerate global catastrophe, because the biosphere could not survive the energy-related and technological tensions that would be created.

This is why the West is seeking a strategy that would make it possible to bypass the current dangerous stage of development at the expense of other countries and without yielding its riches or lowering its own level of consumption. But this goal cannot be achieved without a change in the balance of power.

The withdrawal of the USSR from the world arena destroyed the historically formed geopolitical equilibrium. What then did perestroika and the consequent collapse of the USSR produce? The following changes can be noted:

• our country forfeited its status as a great power and became dependent on external forces;

• we lost all our allies and were forced to curtail cooperation with most of our political and economic partners;

• we experienced a sharp decrease in the level of state and national security in all major areas: military, political, economic, and ideological;

• a strategic destabilization of a huge geographical area has occurred, from the Baltic to the Caucasus and from Kishinev to Dushanbe.

The initiation of plans to establish the "new world order" means that behind-the-scene world forces have started acting decisively to form a rigid, centralized system for controlling the development of human civilization.

The term "new world order" has been around for some time. But only following the Persian Gulf War was this term first tried on the public at large. The bloodbath in Iraq signalled the end of the traditional bipolar world built on the balance between the two superpowers and inaugurated a new era in global politics.

In view of this stark reality, it is clear that our country's foreign policy requires extensive correction. We believe that the concept "healthy national pragmatism" should be the basis of that correction. Within this framework, we should emphasize actions that would bring political and economic benefits for Russia. We should avoid actions for which the country would be compelled to pay a high social, political, or economic price, and we should avoid any actions that could result in direct losses or damage to our country. But this pragmatism should not be allowed to degenerate into unprincipled opportunism, and it should be firmly based on the norms of universal morality and international law.

This doctrine should include the following essential components:

• the continuity of Russia's foreign policy—the new doctrine should absorb all the valuable and positive elements that characterized the international activity of both prerevolutionary Russia and the USSR;

• unconditional independence in making foreign-policy decisions, but not to the exclusion of consultations with other countries;

• reliance on our own resources, without excluding foreign assistance within reasonable limits;

• a rejection of an excessive ideologization of our foreign policy;

• the development of international ties in all parts of the world;

• defensive sufficiency;

• the creation of international conditions offering optimal opportunities for the stable development of our country, the progress of our national economy, and the improvement of the living standard of our people.

The Guarantor of Geopolitical Equilibrium

We must begin by identifying the main probable dangers and obstacles that may block Russia's development. By determining the main threats to our country and civilization, we can define the prime tasks of foreign policy. The proper context for our inquiry would be a historical survey of civilizational and intercivilizational processes and of Russia's historical place and role in these.

Since ancient times, civilizations have been developed, preserved, and moved along by ethnoses—nations and peoples, as well as their broader groupings. The interactions of these powerful influences determine world politics and culture at any given historical moment.

It is clear that history moves in a cyclical, spiral manner. Great minds from Ecclesiastes and Heraclitus, Vico and Leibnitz, Hegel and Marx to Lenin, Toynbee, and Kondratyev have identified many such historical cycles. Some have overlapped, forming "junctures" and "breaking points" of decisive importance, for the explanation of which a number of theories have been developed, such as Lev Gumilyov's theory of "passionary impetuses" and Karl Jaspers's theory of "pivotal time."

All historical theories accept that the development of our own era began two thousand years ago, marking the boundary between the Graeco-Roman civilization and the Christian civilization, which was destined to become the shaping force in global development.

The Roman Empire was the political foundation of this new civilization; its national base was the polyethnic community inherited from the Graeco-Roman Hellenic culture; and the foundation of its social forms of self-organization was the idea of communality and collectivism, stemming from a powerful spiritual tradition in which categories of profit and utility were subordinated to religious-ethical ideals and social morality.

Ten centuries of Russian history attest to the unbroken continuity of the classical Christian civilization and its worldview.

Another event that changed the world and introduced a major influence into history was the emergence of Muslim civilization. This civilization created a powerful center of religious, state, ideological, and cultural attraction that competed with and complemented Christianity. Islam appeared in the seventh century on the Arabian Peninsula among nomadic Arabian tribes and spread quickly throughout the whole southern and eastern parts of the Mediterranean. The tidal wave of Muslim conquest rolled through the Near and Middle East, Central Asia, Africa, and Spain. Islam eventually came to include Turkic peoples, Persians, Africans, and even Slavs.

By the beginning of the second millennium, the destiny of the world began to be decided by the relations among three civilizations: the Orthodox (Byzantine-Slavic), the West European, and the Muslim. Other, often very ancient civilizations did, of course, exist, but by virtue of being self-contained systems, they did not exert a significant influence on the vector of the world's historical development.

From its conception, Western civilization has displayed the ambition to rule. This led to the explosion of military activity known as the Crusades, which shook the European continent for some two centuries.

The Crusades were carried out with the blessings of the Vatican and were aimed not only against the Muslims but also against Orthodox Christians. Apart from capturing and plundering Constantinople, the Byzantine capital, in 1204, there is other ample evidence of the anti-Orthodox antagonism of Western civilization. In 1147, Pope Eugene III blessed the "first German crusade against the Slavs." The long and bloody struggle of militarized Catholic monastic orders against the northwestern lands of Orthodox Russia bears witness to the realization of that blessing.

Western civilization went through a number of epochs: the Renaissance (fourteenth and fifteenth centuries), the Reformation (sixteenth and seventeenth centuries), great geographical discoveries, the Age of Enlightenment (eighteenth century), and the Industrial Revolution (nineteenth century). The twentieth century brought the epoch of catastrophes.

The West's attempts to perpetuate global primacy have not always been based on political strategies anchored in the dynamics and mechanisms of civilizational changes. The more astute Western geopoliticians have recognized this. In 1993, the journal *Foreign Affairs* published an article by Professor Samuel Huntington of Harvard University, "The Clash of Civilizations." Huntington believes that world politics is now entering a new phase, in which the basic source of conflicts will be neither ideologies nor economics. Instead, future conflicts will be caused by cultural-historical differences and the collisions of civilizations. The shape of the world, according to Huntington, will be defined progressively more by the interaction of seven or eight main civilizations. He identifies these civilizations as Western, Slavic-Orthodox, Confucian (Chinese), Hindu, Japanese, Latin-American, and African. He expects most serious and bloody conflicts to occur along the fault lines dividing these civilizations. He declares that today the old methodology of geopolitical forecasts based on the classification of states according to their ideology (communism–capitalism), political system (democracy–totalitarianism), or economic system (free market–state regulation) no longer meets the requirements of our time.

Huntington believes that the basic strength of each civilization will be defined by its military power. Accordingly, the West should do everything possible to check the military development of "potentially hostile civilizations" by curtailing their armament. Alternatively, the West should expand the territorial borders of its civilization at the expense of the states of Eastern Europe and Latin America. As for Russia and Japan, he believes that in both countries Western priority support should be given to those groupings that favor the Western model of development. It is obvious that Huntington's belief in the inevitability of escalation stems from his concern for preserving the global domination of the West. Our position is quite different.

We recognize that the contradictions and collisions among civilizations may well become the determining factor of world and regional instability. But to us it seems more probable that intercivilizational rivalries will be expressed in their accustomed and already "tested" ways and forms. We reject the fallacious "inevitability" of the Armageddon scenario that Huntington seems to predict.

The most serious, painful, and widespread rifts that have influenced world politics are the following:

- geopolitical (Atlanticism–Eurasia);
- socioeconomic (wealthy North–poor South);
- racial and ethnic (interethnic);
- confessional (interreligious);
- intrasystemic, within the framework of related cultures.

Given these disparities and conditions, the efforts required to sustain a leading position in the world would undermine the internal viability of even the richest nation. The absence of a second global "power center" would inevitably result in a geopolitical configuration that would present the West with new problems that are impossible to solve within the framework of the "new world order."

Only those peoples, societies, and cultures that have been able to attain territorial self-sufficiency—that is, geopolitical self-reliance—can claim real independence and sovereignty.

As a consequence of the global standoff between the Atlantic (United States + Western Europe) and the Eurasian (USSR + Eastern Europe) blocs, all other regions of the planet were pulled into the magnetic fields of the rival superpowers. But today formerly inactive alternative power centers are gradually increasing their influence on world politics.

History has evolved in such a manner that most of the competing Large Spaces, that is, territorially, economically, and culturally self-sufficient regions of the planet, coincide with the "homes" of the major modern civilizations (Russia, India, and China are examples). Strong centripetal and consolidating tendencies are on the rise in civilizations as yet lacking political (state) and geographical coherence—for example, the Muslim world.

Under these circumstances, it is important for Russia to develop its own prudent global strategy while quickly adapting to the changes in the world arena. Russia's unique geographical position, coupled with its considerable military-economic, demographic, and political capabilities, dictates a special type of development for our foreign policy. We should strive to return to Russia its traditional centuries-long role as keeper and guarantor of the world's geopolitical balance.

National Interests

Feasible directions in which Russian national interests may develop depend, in our view, on several "typical" global scenarios. And, although it is highly unlikely that any scenario could come to pass in a "chemically pure" form, three variants of intercivilizational interaction are nevertheless concentrated expressions of the tendencies now shaping the development of the human community.

Today, the primary factors that influence geopolitical dynamics consist of three basic categories: "factors of the new world order," "factors of risk," and "factors of stabilization." With reference to these categories, the most probable scenarios of future world politics could be characterized as follows:

- the scenario of the "new world order" (NWO);
- the scenario of a "global time of troubles"; or
- the scenario of a "balance of interests."

Let us consider each in some detail.

The "New World Order" Scenario

It is clear today that the plan for the "new world order" is nothing more than the use of old mondialistic techniques aimed at establishing a global dictatorship of the West to preserve the illusion of its political, economic, and military leadership.

But in its finished form, this plan represents a far more complex and multidimensional phenomenon. This plan is a global, messianic, and religious project that is far larger in scope and better prepared than the Roman imperialism of Tiberius and Diocletian, the Abbasid caliphate, the Protestant Reformation in Europe, or the Trotskyists' dream of World Revolution.

As its philosophical base, the NWO uses "post-Christian" religiosity. Its ideology (see "The End of History" by Francis Fukuyama) promises to realize the centuries-old, messianic hopes of the West to create a liberal democratic "paradise on earth." The nonsecular ideologues of mondialism are convinced that the Messiah is coming soon to establish the laws of a perfect religion on earth and to usher in a "golden age" for the world governed by a single World Supergovernment.

These views appear with increasing frequency in statements by members of the Bilderberg Club, the Trilateral Commission, the American Council on Foreign Relations, and other centers of mondialism. Influential Western religious sects, such as Jehovah's Witnesses and Seventh Day Adventists, teach their followers to expect just such events. Although some may regard such thinking as paranoid doomsaying or intellectually vacuous religiosity, such views may have influence on the colder realities of political life, social policy, and economic development.

Geopolitically, the NWO is tied to the "global strategy" of the United States and the concept of the Larger Atlantic Space. It is here that internal "highly organized spaces" of the so-called Trade System will be concentrated. According to some published accounts of this version of the future, "power will be measured by the quantity of money controlled," which will become a "uniform equivalent and a universal measure of things." This is how Jacques Attali, a former director of the European Bank for Reconstruction and Development and a member of the Bilderberg Club, describes it in his recent book *Lines of the Horizon*.[19]

Economically, the NWO epitomizes a kingdom of the "free market," where "money will determine the law" and "a person will be an object and a commodity." Culturally and nationally, the ideology of the NWO stands for a discordant mix of different cultural heritages—a concept against which Konstantin Leontyev fought ferociously years ago. A mass culture of huge megalopolises and boundless cosmopolitanism of "ethnic melting pots"—these are the ideals promoted by the NWO.

The "Global Time of Troubles" Scenario

This scenario is the antithesis to the NWO. It is to go into effect if the mondialistic utopia of the West falls by the wayside. Many people, from Zbigniew Brzezinski in the United States to Metropolitan Ioann in Russia, consider this to be a feasible eventuality.[20]

The threat of an explosion is inherent in Western consumer civilization itself. For hundreds of years, this civilization has advocated material well-being, rejecting "ideal" goals that did not promise direct material gains and superprofits. But today, production can be expanded only if the volume of natural resources and manpower involved in the economic cycle constantly continues to increase. From century to century, the West has sucked in minerals and cheap colonial labor, new territories and spheres of influence, goods, money, ideas, and brains. The mechanism is so constructed that it simply cannot stop; stopping would mean the end of the dominance of the West.

Even a reduction in the rate of growth causes serious intrasystemic crises. And a significant reduction in consumption with a collateral lowering of standards of living would break the "free world" into smithereens. The urgent need to delay the inevitable day of radical change—the halting of the mechanism—motivates the West increasingly to separate itself from the rest of humankind.

The collapse of the West would cause a chain reaction worldwide. All fault lines will break open, "hot points" will flare up, and conflicting regions will be engulfed in flames. If this were to occur, Russia could save itself from total chaos and global disaster only if it works in advance to strengthen its state system and its ideological, political, economic, and military self-sufficiency.

The "Balance of Interests" Scenario

The "balance of interests" scenario assumes that the collapse of the West will take place not all at once but as the end of a process of decline. In this case, there is hope that a new global political infrastructure could be established during the transition period. A system of regional "centers of power," with each center having its own sphere of geopolitical responsibility, should be able to find and maintain a mutually acceptable balance of interests.

In this scenario, a renewed Russia would be able to be the guarantor of this "balanced world."

Already existing structures for world cooperation, such as the United Nations, could help in the creation of such a global model. However, as a prerequisite, these structures would have to undergo a "de-Americanization" and move out from under the influence of the mondialistic West. A real opportunity could then emerge to use the experience of various international institutions as a foundation for the creation of independent and neutral mechanisms for developing mutually acceptable solutions and for coordinating cooperation.

However, such a "balanced world" will, of course, not automatically become a world without conflicts and problems. Therefore, it is especially important that the "balanced world" be based on a geopolitical equilibrium of the Large Areas, civilizations, and ethnic-confessional "centers of power" and on a recognition of the legitimate interests of all states and peoples.

State Security

The mechanism for maintaining a strategy for state security includes diverse means and measures. Let us now analyze one of its key components—the military doctrine of the Russian Federation. In our view, the military-political problems that this doctrine must address can be summarized as follows:

1. A qualitatively changed geopolitical and military-strategic situation requires that we radically rethink the military doctrine of the Soviet period, which was based on the bipolar balance of forces. We must reject any unreasonable geopolitical ambitions that would exhaust our economy. These ambitions were frequently dictated not by national, state, or historical interests but by ideological postulates. We need to reorient our armed forces to be ready to act against regional threats to our security. We must continue to maintain a level of our military potential that would guarantee "unacceptable injury" to any potential aggressor.

Simultaneously, we must ensure the historical continuity of our "defensive-patriotic mentality"—from military-political theory to military-strategic practice. This means recognizing that Russia's security can be guaranteed only if our armed forces are ready to resist the whole spectrum of potential power threats—from global to regional, local, and even internal pressures and incursions.

2. Our blueprints for military construction should reflect and be ready to counter the disturbing tendencies of international politics, all of which promise Russia nothing but new worries, alarms, and diverse threats. Thus, our readiness to resist such threats with force, along with a peacemaking policy sufficient to prevent dangerous situations from forming, represents the most effective way of guaranteeing Russia's security.

3. Russia's current military strategy can be characterized as a strategy of "defensive sufficiency" based on the political premise of "healthy national pragmatism." This means that:

• the current period should be considered as a time of stabilization, during which it will above all be necessary to minimize the social, economic, and military damage inflicted on our country over the past few years;

• we must develop mechanisms for mobilizing all of society's resources to take our country rapidly out of its deep systemic crisis;

• we must ensure priority attention to internal problems of social recovery and national revival;

• we must reduce our external state activity to a minimum and even withdraw from any supranational organization that claims the right to intervene in the domestic affairs of sovereign states;

• we must limit the military activity of our armed forces to protecting our national interests and ensure that the armed forces have the required technical, organizational, and legal resources to carry out this task;

• the material and personnel resources channeled into national defense should be determined with a view to the importance of preventing a further deterioration of Russia's military-political and military-strategic positions in the world arena.

The events of the past few years have demonstrated that Russia has no reliable military allies. Accordingly, our military construction should ensure that the armed forces will be able to repel direct military aggression against Russia and also respond to regional threats.

4. Along with the concepts "healthy national pragmatism" and "defensive sufficiency," Russia's military doctrine should also include such key concepts as "vital interests" and "potential opponent."

It would make sense to introduce the use of the latter term in place of the term "probable opponent," which was discredited during the cold war and referred to states or alliances of states considered hostile on ideological grounds. The concept "potential opponent" has no such bias. It is ideologically neutral and reflects hypothetical situations in accordance with justified military-political conclusions.

The presence of potential military threats in the contemporary world cannot be ignored. The proposed use of the term "potential opponent" should not alarm anyone or reflect negatively on the defensive character of our military doctrine.

The concept "vital interests" will add more clarity and direction to the process of military construction, especially in terms of those issues not adequately covered by the term "potential opponent." These "vital interests," which are understood as Russia's legitimate right to strive for a geopolitical or regional balance of forces that would ensure its security and territorial integrity, may include regions where there is no "potential opponent." The concept of "vital interests" can also serve as a basis for our military policy where friendly relations with local states, mutual loyalty, or similar factors exclude the possibility of any other view of a situation and require a flexible approach to ensuring Russia's security.

Alternative Strategy

The twentieth century witnessed a global standoff between two social systems—capitalism and socialism. Yet the real contradictions and problems of humankind's development, reflected in this dispute, remain unresolved.

Capitalism has changed unrecognizably in the five centuries of its existence, but it has retained its essential characteristics. Thus, production in general as the eternal and natural precondition of human life continues to have the concrete-historical form of production of value and added value—capital, which has no internal measure and must always aspire to infinite quantitative growth. But resolving the whole complex of humankind's current problems is impossible by way of transforming the Western consumer society into a global model of development.

Only two strategies remain feasible.

The first is a neo-Malthusian model and calls for a limitation of growth or even a complete conservation of the level of mass production. The existing world structure of distribution and consumption, which perpetuates the division of mankind into the "golden billion" and the raw-material peripheries exploited by it, corresponds socioeconomically to this strategy. Politically, this strategy presupposes the global hegemony of the advanced capitalist countries in the form of the "new world order."

The other strategy is aimed at a further development of productive forces and a steady increase in the well-being of the entire world population. It provides for the preservation of ecological balance by a qualitative change in the pattern of production and consumption. It entails a radical revision of social value systems and of the priorities of economic development and an appropriate reorientation of the general vector of scientific and technological progress.

The aggregate of ideas and plans being developed in many countries of the world has come to be known generally as the concept of "steady development." Regardless of the specific technical and organizational details of this concept, its social content and the world-historical mission for its realization are identified with the modern form of socialism, which corresponds to the new development level of productive forces and to the problems now facing humankind.

Socialism's development has approached a turning point. The epoch of early proletarian revolutions, which was a direct reaction to the decay of imperialism and to the material and moral catastrophes of world wars, has essentially completed its cycle. These revolutions have fulfilled their historical role by breaking the fetters of world imperialism and ushering in the first socialist states on the one hand and, on the other, by stimulating global reform in the advanced capitalist countries, thus leading to the affirmation of the socioeconomic rights and political freedoms of working people and speeding up the transition of capitalism into a "consumer society."

The socialist revolution in Russia was not an idle "Bolshevik experiment" but the people's only chance for national-state survival in the face of economic collapse, territorial disintegration, and the rule of a socially inept bourgeois-landowner bloc.

From the devastations caused by World War I and the civil war that followed, a program for stable development—the New Economic Policy (NEP)—was inaugurated. But because of external threats to Russia, the program had to be modified radically. All the resources of a planned economy were mobilized under the slogan "Catch up with and surpass!" The accelerated accumulation of primary capital characteristic of capitalist industrialization was carried out at the expense of the peasantry with the broad use of compulsory, often free, labor in an atmosphere of military discipline and appeals to revolutionary asceticism.

After the problem of direct survival was solved and the time came to build socialism on its own foundations, a crude simplification of the socialist idea was permitted to occur. The essentially correct slogan calling for the "maximum satisfaction of the growing needs of the working people" remained at the level of an abstract, anti-historical understanding of the capabilities and needs of people and of their connection with production. Public "wealth" and "progress" were equated with their bourgeois form—the "accumulation of goods" and the boundless multiplication of these goods. As a result, the Third CPSU Program, adopted in 1961, added no new impetus to the old slogan "Catch up with and surpass!" and amounted to no more than an uncritical imitation of the Western "society of consumption."

As a result, the alternative of using a technical-economic maneuver to bypass this stage and enter a qualitatively new road of steady development using the advantages of a planned system and employing new technological capabilities remained unrecognized and unused. By losing this opportunity, socialism lost its historical perspective.

This loss was predetermined by the absolutization of the experience of early socialist transformations, during which socialism concentrated its main efforts on overcoming the capitalist form of property ownership and distribution but left intact the capitalist way of production and consumption with its corresponding system of social values and priorities. Without first resolving this striking anomaly, the historical mission of socialism—the socialization of production and the development on its basis of higher incentives for labor and creativity, of genuine social justice, and of conditions for the fulfillment of each person—could not be carried out.

The creation of a model of steady development, in this way giving socialism its second wind, is not a purely technical problem but is rather characterized by on organic unity of interconnected socioeconomic, political, cultural-psychological, and technological aspects.

The global situation dictates that humankind ensure a harmonization of the rates and characteristics of society's development and find a strategy that will preserve the natural environment and material and labor resources. Even now it is possible to draw the general contours of a technological basis for steady development, which will be characterized by the following:

• the continued improvement of automated management systems, the accumulation and transfer of information (microelectronics, optic-wave engineering, global information networks, "artificial intelligence"), the development of new energy sources and means for storing and transferring them (controlled thermonuclear synthesis, high-temperature superconductivity), the mastering of new methods of processing raw materials (coherent radiation with a high density of energy flow, cryogenic engineering), and the mastering of new natural processes (microbiology, advanced chemistry);

• the transition from conveyor serial production to flexible automated manufacture, and the individualization of production and consumption;

• the deconcentration of production capacities, and de-urbanization on the basis of improving transport and telecommunications systems;

• increased safety as a comprehensive feature of human–machine systems, encompassing all technical, sociopsychological, and cultural-moral aspects;

• a new approach to designing technical systems—increasing their efficiency, flexibility, and service life; removing contradictions between functional and physical depreciation by constantly modernizing and retargeting products;

• overcoming ecological restrictions by unifying production and nature-reconstruction processes into an integrated technological process; whereas until now nature has served as a seemingly eternal and inexhaustible "well" of human labor ("industrial" type of technology), now labor should be transformed into the basis for the preservation of the natural environment("postindustrial" type of technology).

In its socioeconomic transformation, the technological process coincides with the process of the real socialization of labor (that is, the strengthening of its collective character), with the expansion of interconnections among various branches and sectors of production, and with an increase in the manageability level of production and in its subordination to general state and global goals and control. The socialization of labor is the "main material foundation for the inevitable advent of socialism" (V. Lenin), for the gradual elimination of the vices of private ownership, and for the overcoming of the negative effects of an uncontrolled market through scientific regulation.

Without doubt, a decisive role in the technological breakthrough to the model of steady development will be played by a large-scale public sector regulated by the state and belonging to the working majority of people.

The global, human character of the strategy of steady development assumes that each country and each people will find its own path for reaching this goal. The future of humankind lies not in shallow unification but in the unity that comes from diversity and a fruitful interaction among unique social organisms.

A secure future can only be built on a solid foundation of time-tested tradition and by clearly recognizing the unique characteristics of our history, our fate, the nature of arising problems, and the principles and goals that must underlie a promising model of development.

Under today's conditions of social contradiction and extreme stress, we are in particular need of a national and state idea that is capable of turning into a material force, of uniting around itself all healthy patriotic forces, and of giving intelligent purpose to the activity of the broadest strata of society.

The author sees Russia as a special world, a complete "social cosmos" with specific historical, geopolitical, philosophical, national, and economic features in which the general laws of social development are refracted in a unique way. The current Russian Federation is not yet fully Russia but a "rump" with bloody, severed connections. The main reason for our sociopolitical ailment is the attempt at capitalist restoration, which has undermined the material and spiritual foundations of our society and state and is making the vast differences between Western civilization and Russian civilization ever more apparent. Capitalism is inconsistent with the flesh and blood, with the being, with the habits, and with the psychological makeup of our society. Capitalism once led our society to a civil war, and now it will not take root in Russian soil.

It is time for everyone, especially those who have political power, to realize the incompatibility of capitalism with the national mentality of Russians so as not to be forced later to have bitter regrets about missed opportunities and unforeseen losses. Therefore, as the Program of the Communist Party of the Russian Federation stresses, "the rebirth of our Fatherland and the return to the path of socialism are inseparable. History has given the peoples of our Motherland the same choice as in 1917 and in 1941: either a great power and socialism, or our country's further disintegration and final transformation into a colony."

Russia has had enough revolutionary upheavals. But that does not mean that Russians have agreed to the role of a victim to be sacrificed for their neighbors' well-being. Most of our citizens prefer purely peaceful means for returning Russia to a path of stable development rather than the madness of the portended slaughter. For them this development is one in which the measure of well-being is not the self-indulgence of the so-called "new Russians," who have nothing in common with age-old Russian values, but rather man himself and his vital needs, in keeping with the immortal formula for the progress of all humankind: the free development of each is a prerequisite for the free development of all.

Editor's Notes

1. Ilya Muromets (Ilya of Murom) is a legendary hero of Russian epic poems.

2. I. Ilin, *About a Future Russia* (New York: Hermitage, 1991), p. 152 (in Russian).

3. Nikita Khrushchev (1894–1971) was in power from 1958 to 1964. Alexei Kosygin (1904–1980) was the prime minister of the USSR from 1964 to 1980. Yuri Andropov (1914–1984) was the top Soviet leader from 1982 to 1984.

4. Reference is to the agreement to dissolve the Soviet Union.

5. Nikolai Danilevsky (1822–1885) and Konstantin Leontyev (1831–1891) were Russian sociologists and philosophers who promoted ideas of pan-Slavism.

6. The writings of these conservative religious philosophers were banned in the Soviet Union.

7. Oswald Spengler (1880–1936) was a German existentialist philosopher. His famous book was published in the 1920s. He is quoted here from the Russian translation of his book.

8. The reference here is to the controversial article by Francis Fukuyama, an American author, in the journal *The National Interest* (Summer 1989).

9. Gumilyov invented this term to refer to critical periods of history. See his book *Ancient Rus* (Moscow, 1992), in Russian.

10. Mikhail Gorchakov (1798–1883) was a Russian statesman and diplomat.

11. In Soviet central planning, the designations "group A" and "group B" stood for heavy and light industry, respectively. "Group A" included armaments.

12. Academician Andrei Sakharov (1921–1992) was a leading advocate of democratic reforms and human rights.

13. War communism refers to an early period in Soviet history (1918–21) that was marked by the extremely harsh conditions of Lenin's dictatorial rule.

14. This is a reference to the suppression of recalcitrant parliamentarians led by Speaker Ruslan Khasbulatov, who refused to disband when Yeltsin dismissed the parliament and called for new elections. On Yeltsin's orders, the parliament building, known as the White House, was attacked by artillery and tanks on October 3, 1993.

15. Approximately 65 percent of voters wanted to keep the union (March 17, 1991).

16. This is a reference to the plot to remove Mikhail Gorbachev from power in August 1991.

17. Grigory Rasputin (1872–1916) was the confidant and spiritual adviser of Tsar Nicholas II.

18. Sergei Uvarov (1786–1855) was a Russian statesman under Nicholas I.

19. Jacqus Attali's books (in French) deal mostly with West European and NATO politics.

20. Metropolitan Ioann was the late head of the Russian Orthodox Church in Leningrad/St. Petersburg. He was known for his extreme Russian nationalism.

Part 4

What Is to Be Done?

The Communist Economic Program and Election Platform

Presented here are the two main policy documents used by Zyuganov during the summer 1996 presidential election campaign. They offer a blueprint of the administration and development of Russia under the auspices of Zyuganov and his opposition colleagues if and when they come to power.

—V.M.

The Economic Program, June 1996

1. The Outcome of the Reforms Being Implemented Today: On the Brink of National Catastrophe

The results of Yeltsin's governing are catastrophic. Never before has our country sustained in time of peace such a destructive blow to the national economy—industrial output has been halved. The most severe losses have been suffered by the previously most advanced, progressive, and promising sectors: machine building, instrument and machine-tool making, and the electronic, electrical, light, and food industries. Our agriculture is rapidly disintegrating, and living standards have declined precipitously, resulting in a sharp social polarization into the very rich and the very poor.

Our country is on the verge of social explosion. By all significant indexes, Russia has been pushed back by many years. The promises of the authorities are no longer believed by anyone, and their inability and incapacity to manage Russia's national economy effectively and professionally is obvious to everyone. The choice today is either a change in economic policy or national catastrophe.

What should this new policy be? It must be modern and national, that is, it must incorporate and reflect all the newest tendencies of world development, take into account our country's traditions, and respond to our national interests. Such a policy would then enjoy the broadest support of the Russian people, and Russia would then be able to recover quickly from its crisis and regain its former position in the world.

2. Reasons for the Economic Collapse: The Neutron Bomb of Monetarism

In order to find the best way out of the crisis, we must first determine what caused it. We must decide the model for recovery best suited to our reality: our own NEP, Franklin D. Roosevelt's New Deal, or the models of post–World War II Germany or Japan? In its main characteristics, the current situation in Russia resembles most the Great Depression in the United States in 1929–33: both there then and in our country now, economic collapse was caused not by postwar ruin but by major breakdowns in the functioning of systems for managing and regulating the national economy. And in both cases production declines were caused not by the physical destruction of production capacities but by the shrinking of effective demand and by the irrational use of financial and credit resources.

To be sure, the degree of our decline far exceeds not only the Great Depression in the United States but also the impact on our country of the most terrible world war in history. In our case, this very deep crisis was brought on by the fundamental defectiveness not simply of individual management decisions but of the ideology on which the policy being pursued rested—a vulgarized version of monetarism and economic "shock therapy." This entire arsenal of methods, fashioned by experts from international financial organizations exclusively for use in developing and dependent countries, has never been applied to any developed country and has never produced positive results. This policy is based on an extremely primitive approach: less government—less government expenditures and less money in circulation—a smaller budget deficit—lower inflation—more investment. All attempts to follow this mythic formula, both former and present, have done nothing but ruin our country's production, rob our people, and force many to go hungry.

What is the reason for this failure? Money is the lifeblood of the economy. The supply of domestic currency should therefore be sufficient for the normal functioning of the national economy's organism: both for the operational budgets of enterprises (to buy raw materials and everything else that is essential for production) and for individual citizens in the form of salaries, pensions, assistance payments (to buy goods and services). But our woeful reformers, out of the whole wealth of world economic theories and practices, have adopted the one, "only true" monetarist theory of Milton Friedman, according to which it is enough for the government to refrain from giving anyone any money and from interfering in anything for everything to take care of itself. With their one and only idea of an unconditional reduction of the amount of money in circulation in the name of the sacred idol of "financial stabilization," these people are like the medieval healers who knew only bloodletting. Our ailing economy is near death because of their "treatment," but they continue to prescribe more of the same medicine.

As a result, people who receive their often delayed salaries and pensions can buy less and less. Enterprises, deprived of operational funds and unable to sell their output (because of decreased demand), are forced to cut production drastically or even stop it, giving their workers long administrative leaves or firing them. Our factories and plants, research laboratories and construction bureaus, fields and farms are becoming idle and empty. Russia appears to have been hit by a neutron bomb: buildings, machinery, and equipment remain intact, but the people have disappeared. Domestic production is coming to a halt, and domestic goods are being replaced by imported goods, which are freely admitted to the Russian market, now turned into what amounts to a dumping ground. To pay for these imports, the Yeltsin administration is going into debt and the whole country is living on credit. A vicious circle has been formed: no money—no production, no production —no money.

The government counted on private investments, which the minister of the economy promised a year ago would be pouring in, but these expectations proved to be groundless. As could have been expected, chanting empty monetaristic incantations brought negative results. The illusions are gone, and it has become clear that we have only one effective lever—the state. Today, even foreign experts estimate that the degree of government participation in the regulation of the economies of developed countries is 40–50 percent. But in Russia it has gone down to 15–20 percent—in spite of the fact that we have no developed market infrastructures, the level of monopolization in our national economy is high, and historically the state has always played a very large role in economic life. Today, therefore, only the state can pull our national economy out of its crisis and correct the huge distortions and disproportions that have been formed or that have increased drastically during recent years. The most serious of these distortions is the effort to turn Russia's economy into an energy and raw materials supplier of a colonial, supplementary, and dependent type.

3. Ways to Avoid Economic Colonization: Not Russia for Gazprom but Gazprom for Russia

Even before the onset of the "reforms," our economy depended too much on its energy, raw-materials, and extracting branches. Now this one-sidedness is much worse: while the processing industries recently experienced a further drop of 10 percent, the share of the extracting industries grew by the same percentage. The policy of extracting and exporting energy resources in exchange for imported finished goods defies all modern world experience. The discrepancy in world prices between raw materials and finished products has been constantly growing in favor of the latter. The same amount of crude oil buys progressively less finished goods. This tendency is growing and is leading us as a country not toward wealth but toward poverty. Our growing dependency on imports is making the prospect of the loss of our national independence more and more likely. A country that serves as a raw-materials appendage has no future. The policy pursued by most oil-exporting countries is to use petro-dollars to develop their own domestic production.

Saudi Arabia, for example, has created, even in its extremely unfavorable natural conditions, a highly effective agriculture. And what about Russia? In 1994, we received 16 billion dollars more for what we sold abroad than we spent on purchases there. In 1995, this difference was already 20 billion dollars, a 25 percent increase in a single year. But, amazingly enough, our capital investments for the same period decreased by 13 percent. What happened to the money if the one-year surplus of exports over imports alone equals two three-year credit allotments from the International Monetary Fund? What sense does it make to increase the sale of our natural resources if the revenue is not invested in the national economy but evaporates "in unknown directions"?

These directions are in fact well known, as can be seen from what happened with the off-budget funds of Gazprom.[1] The funds were spent on building the stupendously supermodern Gazprom headquarters in the southwestern part of Moscow, on paying for the [fall 1995 parliamentary] election campaign of Our Home Is Russia,[2] on purchasing fashionable castles abroad, on secret accounts in foreign banks, and on similar "projects" that are far removed from the interests of our national economy. In the Soviet era, only very limited amounts of petro-dollars were spent to buy imported consumer goods. The rest of the money was used to build new production facilities. Our oilmen used Soviet-made equipment, supporting with their orders our own machine building. And, by the way, they managed to extract more. In 1988, for example, using domestic equipment, we extracted twice as much oil as today. In 1994, Russian oil and gas men spent 4.5 billion dollars—almost 40 percent of their export earnings—to buy foreign equipment, but Russia's domestic factories received no orders from them even though our military-industrial complex, thanks to its high technologies, managed to convert to the production of new equipment for the oil and gas complex to meet world standards.

During the current year, 15 million tons of oil and 20 billion cubic meters of gas have been targeted for export, and the 1 billion dollars in expected earnings will be used for the purchase of imported equipment for that branch. How long are we going to support foreign machine building while ruining our own? Russian oil and gas, like all our other natural resources, belong to all of Russia, not to the oil and gas "generals," and should for that reason serve all-national interests, not the interests of a branch industry and individual citizens. The state's role in influencing the oil and gas complex and the export of energy resources (through a controlling block of stocks) should therefore be changed.

4. How to Preserve Our Old Positions and Capture New Ones: Breakthrough Strategy

The accelerated development of the processing branches should be based on a two-pronged policy. First, we should recapture our own domestic market for all basic goods with the aid of the protective measures used all over the world: quota systems, tariffs, and so on. We cannot tolerate a situation in which the share of imported goods has risen from 50 percent in 1994 to 88 percent in 1995. The same applies, of course, to the countries of the Commonwealth of Independent States (CIS), especially since Russia continues to subsidize their economies. Experts say that in 1993 about 12 percent of our gross domestic product was used for this purpose. At the beginning of 1996, these republics owed us 9 billion dollars for energy deliveries alone, and there is little reason for optimism about Russia's chances of collecting this money. Russia should clearly be entitled at least to expect a favorable regime for its goods in these markets.

Concurrently, we must broaden our internal market by increasing people's purchasing power through an appropriate income policy and special social programs that meet modern world criteria of social welfare and that restore, as a start, at least the living standards our country enjoyed during the mid-1980s. It is completely unacceptable that the real consumption of the absolute majority of the population has dropped severalfold during the time of the "reforms" and that wages have come to play a peripheral role in incomes, thus sharply lowering the prestige of productive labor and of skills, education, and professional training along with it.

We must remember that all this affects the quality of the labor force, which in today's world is the main resource of an effective and competitive economy. In connection with this, the second direction of our strategy is to capture firm positions in the world market, at least for some of the products of our processing branches. We have certain high-technology lines in which we match or even surpass the world's leaders. These include aviation, space hardware, synthetic materials, armaments, and others. All such production lines must be supported immediately, efforts must be made to retain their uniquely qualified scientific-technical personnel, and their advancement must be stimulated for purposes of retaining and strengthening their position of importance in the world. These must become the skeletal structure of a system of pivotal points of technological growth that will eventually pull our entire national economy to a new technical economic level.

The specific pivotal points for a technological breakthrough must be selected on the basis of scientific expert opinion, resulting in the long-delayed formulation of a clear and precise industrial policy. We must revise fundamentally our attitude toward intellectual property, treating it as a great national asset. The "brain drain" is an unacceptable waste of a vital strategic resource. And it is essential for us to create the material and other conditions that would allow our scientific-production personnel as a group and its members as individuals to realize their potential. Since the intellectual product is derived from the development of the entire infrastructure of science and education, it follows that we must take urgent measures to rebuild scholarship and scientific research at the academies, colleges, and professional schools, making them a high national priority.

5. Can Our Agriculture Be Revived?
Independence in Food Production as a National Priority

All developed countries pay great attention to agriculture, with regular and large government subsidies, financed by taxes, being allocated for its support. Only in our country is agriculture treated as a stepchild. Earlier, during the period of industrialization, the priority given to industry was inevitable since no other means for achieving rapid accumulation were available. But today such a policy is a totally unjustified exploitation. Our agriculture needs a special, preferential credit regime because we are now on the very threshold of losing our national independence.

A huge hidden reserve here is represented by the long chain of parasitic procurement and processing middlemen, who pocket from 80 to 90 percent of the retail price of produce. The actual peasant-producer receives only the remaining 10–20 percent.

Another imperative for state agricultural policy is the liquidation of the discrepancy in domestic prices between industrial and agricultural goods, which may have existed even before the reforms but is now five or six times greater. The price for one liter of gasoline long ago substantially exceeded the price for one liter of milk. And this in an oil-exporting country that is the second largest producer of oil in the world! This unreasonable disparity, which is ruinous for our agricultural sector, must be eliminated immediately.

Our agriculture should be aided without regard for forms of ownership. At the same time, the freedom to buy and sell land is not a prerequisite for raising the efficiency of production, as we can see by the example of many countries where high-technology farming takes place on leased and franchised land. World experience shows that the decisive factor of efficiency is not the form of ownership but technical and organizational conditions.

The state, through its Ministry of Agriculture, should oversee agriculture approximately along the lines of the model used in the United States, where every individual producer signs a contract in advance that provides him with all the means and services needed for production, including bank credits.

An important precondition for raising the efficiency of the agro-industrial complex is infrastructure development in transportation, storage, and processing, which warrants a major investment of funds and efforts.

6. What Should Be Done About Prices? Pricing Reform: Priority Should Be Given to the Producer of Finished Goods

Next to the preferential status of the fuel and energy complex, another anomaly requiring urgent corrective measures is the pricing system. It is difficult to consider normal a situation in which, during the "reforms," prices of finished goods in light industry rose five- to sixfold, transportation rates rose tenfold, and prices of trade services rose twentyfold. Expert calculations show that an equivalent of almost two federal budgets passed through the intermediate trade network. Under current conditions in Russia, price formation is effectively unregulated, and fighting inflation by monetaristic methods alone is ineffective: for every point that the price index goes down, there is a drop in the volume of production of several percentage points.

Real changes occur, as demonstrated by the experiment conducted by the government in late 1995, only when direct state levers are put to use, that is, when prices are fixed. The same can be seen from the experience of other countries, such as the United States during its recovery from the Great Depression.

An accumulated assortment of approved technologies for price regulation has been used at one time or another all over the world, including direct state regulation ("freezing," corridor limits) and indirect actions providing for tariff agreements among all parties involved in production and trade. The specific technology to be used can easily be determined once it has been decided to put price ratios in line with the requirements of improving the competitiveness of our commodity producer.

These requirements are being contradicted most blatantly today by the unjustified superprofits of intermediate traders and by the enormously bloated relative share of costs for raw materials, energy, and transportation in the price of a finished product. It is difficult to explain the absurdity of this situation when many of our prices now match or even exceed parallel world prices. We are losing our competitiveness even in relation to our neighbors. For example, in Ukraine electricity costs half of the release price for Russian producers. As a result, machine builders in Voronezh can import metal from Ukrainian plants for one-third of what it costs to buy it in our own Cherepovets.

Artificially maintaining the rate of the dollar within a fixed corridor while allowing domestic ruble prices to grow freely has benefited only two groups: monopolists of key branches, who have already raised the prices of their products and services by 20–30 percent relative to world prices; and importers, who profit when domestic prices go up while exchange rates remain fixed.

The strategy for developing our own processing industries requires the opposite: strictly limiting trade markups, shortening the intermediary chain, and reducing the relative share of the energy, raw-materials, and transportation component of the price of finished products. What is suggested here would increase the relative share of labor in the cost of production, that is, raise the salaries and wages of workers, which will increase their purchasing power and will thus contribute to the expansion of our domestic market and further stimulate the growth of domestic production.

As compensation for their losses, the key branches (the fuel and energy complex and transportation) should receive direct state subsidies, which have been reduced in recent years (30–fold for railway transport, for example, even though the volume of shipments has shrunk only 2.5–fold). State assistance is an avoidable but justified measure because the rapid decline of the processing branches and the associated loss of markets are causing much greater harm and will continue to do so in the future.

The strategy described here calls for a reconsideration of our attitudes toward Russia's financial resources. In today's world, state revenues as a rule consist of income from state properties, taxes, export, the debts of foreign countries, and people's savings. In general, Russia's economy is characterized by a relatively high level of capital accumulation, approximately 25–28 percent, which is comparable with all developed countries. Thus the absence of needed capital investments is due not to a shortage of internal financial capabilities but to the regime's inability or unwillingness to use national resources to further common national interests.

7. Do We Need State Property?
The State Itself Should Produce Income

One of the main reasons for our economic plight stems from the fact that the Yeltsin team has imposed a policy on our country that directly contradicts the tendencies of current world development. In all developed countries, the role of the state in the economy is growing, as is its share of the national wealth: in the United States, the share of the state's income in gross domestic product increased from 27.6 percent in 1960 to 35.3 percent in 1995; in Japan, from 21.1 percent in 1970 to 34.6 percent in 1994; and in Germany, from 35.5 percent in 1960 to 46.2 percent in 1995.

In Russia, during the first quarter of this year, this indicator was only 17.5 percent. In only a few years of "reform," we have moved rapidly in a direction that is the complete opposite of world development—away from what has come to be known as the modern social state or a socially oriented economy. And, of course, with a state treasury as poor as ours, it is impossible to support science and education, health care and culture, and defense capabilities, not to mention serious social programs, at necessary levels. Our "reforms" are moving us forward into the nineteenth century!

In a poor state, the absolute majority of the population is also poor. To avoid this, the state must itself be an equal subject of market relations and not merely a "night watchman." This is why the state should retain a considerable part of the national production potential, including enterprises in mining, defense, and other branches of industry, transportation, and the energy sector—all of which should form a supporting structure for the national economy, its solid core, its firm base guaranteeing the strategic interests of the state and serving as the main stable source of the treasury's revenues.

The entire assortment of production-organizational forms found in today's world—private, stockholders', cooperative, franchised, medium-sized, small, family-owned, and others—should exist on an equal footing with the state sector and compete with it. They should all be guaranteed equal opportunities on the market of goods and services. It is therefore critically important to develop truly effective measures against any monopolistic tendencies.

State regulatory functions in property relations should be based exclusively on criteria measuring socioeconomic effectiveness and national interests. We must stop the current practice of applying the concept of "political expediency" to purely economic questions. Any state actions affecting economic subject must follow strict legal procedures and be subject to court decisions.

8. What Should Be Done with Taxes?
End Fiscal Madness

The current government is no longer capable of collecting taxes. As of March 1, 1996, unpaid taxes for this year amounted to 40.9 trillion rubles. During the first two months of this year alone, the treasury failed to collect 8 billion dollars in taxes, while at the same time the government was "fighting heroically" trying to get a three-year credit of 10 billion dollars from the International Monetary Fund. This government tries to compensate for its inability to handle the most elementary management tasks by increasing Russia's indebtedness to the West.

Why are taxes not being paid? There are two main reasons.

First is their size, which has long since exceeded all reasonable limits. To survive, every businessman or entrepreneur must seek ways and methods to avoid taxes. In connection with this, a whole branch of professional consultants and agents for hiding income has already emerged.

State agencies have in effect been replaced by criminals and racketeers, who not infrequently also act as arbitrators, charging, of course, "commission fees" for their services. It follows that under existing conditions everyone who is involved in tax collection is vulnerable to pressure from the world of organized crime.

Second, as a result of the frantic efforts to shrink the volume of money in circulation, there is an acute shortage of cash rubles. Dollars and all sorts of substitutes—quasi money in the form of promissory notes, IOU's, barter certificates, and checks of all kinds, so far circulating only inside a given enterprise—are being used to compensate for this chronic shortage. When there is no "normal" money in bank accounts, taxes cannot be collected and payments cannot be made into social funds. So neither the state treasury nor the Pension Fund, for example, gets what it should.

What is to be done?

First, radical tax reform must be initiated immediately. Its main thrust should be to give preferential tax incentives to domestic production, regardless of its form of ownership, while reducing the overall tax burden. Those involved in the production of goods and services, including investments in this sector of the national economy, should receive special tax breaks, not the financial and trading institutions. It is high time for us to understand that a nation cannot go on perpetually selling and reselling the fruits of someone's else labor. What labor is for the individual person, production is for the country as a whole—the only source of material well-being and moral stability.

In accordance with world practices, we should introduce a tax on major fortunes, that is, on properties that have been taken out of the production sphere. By the same token, taxpayers should be made accountable for their incomes as well as for their expenditures. The purpose of this is twofold: to reduce the possibilities of avoiding taxation, and to encourage investments in production rather than consumption. The situation today is such that for all practical purposes the system promotes expenditures for consumption. The absurd result can be readily seen: we have an acute shortage of investments, while at the same time we are breaking world records in terms of the number of expensive cars, jewelry, and real estate in the hands of private citizens!

Second, we should put an end to dogmatic notions about the amount of money in circulation and especially to the practice of resolving this issue according to the requirements of the International Monetary Fund. Methods for determining how much domestic currency is needed to service a given economy have long been known and have been approved by world practice. These methods are the ones that should be used in our policy on the issuance of money, keeping in mind the need to get foreign currencies and all kinds of money surrogates out of circulation as quickly as possible. Naturally, this should be done in conjunction with the strategy of targeted production crediting, that is, financial-credit policy and industrial policy should be interconnected.

9. What Should We Do with Foreign Capital?
Investments, Not Credits

The main thing is to start governing Russia in our own interests, in the interests of our own national economy, our own state, and our own nation. This does not, of course, mean that we should refuse to pay our debts, but we should refrain from multiplying them in the future.

Our president and the current government are good at only one thing: begging all over the world and then spending the solicited dollars abroad on purchases of foreign goods for the purpose of eating through them. They resemble a hopeless alcoholic, who begs from all his neighbors, sells everything in his house for a pittance just to get a drink, and has no concern for what tomorrow will bring.

The IMF loan is terrifying not only because it will be a burden on us, our children, and our grandchildren. It is terrifying because we have used as collateral our independence and our right to be masters in our own house. Nothing like this has ever happened to Russia before. Here is an example: The International Monetary Fund promised to lend Russia a little over a billion dollars by the time of the presidential elections in June. But one of the conditions is that we must cancel export tariffs on oil that we sell abroad. This will cost us 1.5 billion dollars! Thus, we stand to lose more than we borrowed. Moreover, as a result there will be a new hole in our state budget. How will we patch it up? "No problem," says our government, "we are introducing an excise tax—that is, another domestic tax—on gasoline and raising the price of electricity. Let our citizens and enterprises fork it out and make up the difference."

This is not how things should be done. We have before us the example of China: however much production is declining in Russia, it is going up by the same percentage points annually in China. How can this be? There are many reasons, but one is that the Chinese deal not with international financial organizations (whose interests are not so much economic as political) but with individual foreign entrepreneurs. These entrepreneurs are not lending money to China's government with interest and on condition but investing their capital—building plants and factories, selling modern technologies, and creating joint ventures. In this situation everyone wins: the foreign co-owners, the Chinese workers whom they employ, and China's government, which taxes their profits. Such infusions of foreign capital are truly beneficial for the countries in which they are invested.

Strangely enough, foreigners are not afraid to invest money in the People's Republic of China, even though it is ruled by communists. China occupies second place in the world in the volume of foreign investments: over the past ten years, 129 billion dollars have been invested by foreigners in China, compared to only 6 billion in Russia. We are the only country in the world in which the volume of IMF credits has exceeded the volume of private foreign direct investments. This is why China's market is moving forward while ours is rolling back.

What we should do is create the right conditions for foreign businessmen and give them guarantees, as they do in the rest of the world. Above all, there need to be legal guarantees, which require that we adopt a law on nationalization that would clearly specify in what instances, under what conditions, and following what legal procedure nationalization could take place, what compensation the owner receives, and so forth. Such laws exist in almost every other country, and no one need worry about his property: with such a law in place, only a court has the right to make decisions affecting property, not politicians. Property is guaranteed by the entire legal system of the country, including the Constitutional Court and the Supreme Court.

But the main guarantee is to have peaceful, stable sociopolitical conditions in the country. How is this achieved? Of course, not by believing official incantations that the party of power should and will stay in office one more term. A country is secure when its people live well and when prosperity grows from one year to the next. But when people are hungry today and can expect nothing good from tomorrow, their country cannot be secure and stable. The only guarantee is a real and visible improvement in the lives of all our citizens, not just of a handful of those who got "lucky."

10. Why Is the Treasury Empty?
You Cannot Carry Water in a Sieve

There are two sides to the problem of financial resources: how to collect money, and how to use it effectively. At this time in Russia, budgetary funds are being used effectively only to make personal fortunes, which are quickly exported. Here are a few recent examples.

The Accounting Office found that commercial banks regularly "turn over" the money of Russian taxpayers and reap the interest. As a result, the state budget is short 7–12 trillion rubles every month. The same office exposed a huge racket involving federal money earmarked for the purchase of food. The Federal Production Corporation, which was specially created for this purpose, "hijacked" many trillions of rubles through the commercial firms affiliated with it, and this money is now irretrievably lost.

According to an investigation by the military procurator's office, since July 1994, more than 150 billion rubles, including bank interest, allocated for the construction of housing for military personnel were lost or stolen in the process of being credited without authorization to various commercial structures. This represents three-quarters of all the funds the Ministry of Defense received from the state budget for housing.

The director of the Federal Employment Office illegally deposited 15.4 billion rubles in commercial banks instead of in the Bank of Russia, which pays higher interest. Judging by what we already know, it is hard even to imagine what will surely be revealed about the misuse of funds in Chechnya.

What do the cited examples have in common? Every one involves money from the federal budget and commercial structures (banks, firms). The conclusion is obvious: it is pointless to expect the situation to change without establishing order in the use of budget funds. No matter now much tax money is collected, under current conditions it will leak from the sieve of the state treasury into private pockets. The practice of using commercial banks to collect and handle budget funds needs serious revision. Otherwise, we are doomed to trying endlessly to fill up a reservoir from which money leaks continuously, with much of it ending up abroad.

We must stop the flow of capital out of the country. Experts estimate that approximately 300 billion dollars have been taken out of the country and deposited in the West. This figure is growing by 1.5 billion dollars a month, which is equivalent to one-half of the annual credit we receive from the International Monetary Fund.

We must adopt extremely urgent and strict measures to block all channels for siphoning our national financial resources out of the country. We should put in place more effective controls over the distribution and use of hard-currency reserves by commercial banks and of the hard-currency earnings of exporting enterprises. As for the funds that are already abroad, their holders should be offered a limited amnesty period on the condition that they return their funds to Russia and invest them in the production sector.

11. Where to Start and Where Are the Reserves? Start the Motor and the Fuel Will Be Found

The best practical package of measures to start pulling Russia out of economic crisis may include the following. First, we jump-start our light industry by extending targeted preferential credit to it to form working capital, so that our textile factories in Ivanovo, for example, will no longer have to look for British middlemen to buy cotton from Uzbekistan. Concurrently, we must raise import duties and apply other nontariff measures to stop the unchecked access of low-quality goods from abroad to our market.

By doing this, we would stand a good chance of rapidly raising our tax revenue. After all, it is in the textile and other light industries that we have experienced the largest production slumps: during the past five years the production of textiles has gone down fivefold; and knit-wear, clothing, and footwear seven- to elevenfold. As a result, the revenue received from the textile and light industries dropped from 26.4 percent of the state budget in 1990 to only 2 percent in 1995. Just by bringing this one branch of industry back to its former level of full capacity, we could increase budget revenues by more than 20 percent. At the same time, the state would be relieved from spending money on unemployment programs and unemployment compensation in Russia's textile belt, which today is a disaster area.

Another effective source of finances is a positive foreign trade balance, that is, a significant surplus of earnings from exports over spending on imports. Last year, our exports exceeded imports by about 20 billion dollars. But this money was spent on nonproduction consumption, was deposited in foreign banks and companies, or was invested in real estate in Paris and London suburbs. By revamping the structure of imports and reducing the demand for imported goods, most of which can be produced domestically, we could expect an even more favorable balance of trade.

The third important source of revenue would be a return to the state monopoly on alcohol. Ten years ago, "vodka money" comprised more than 30 percent of budget revenues, compare with only 1.5 percent last year. While drinking has actually increased, the state has lost in the vodka trade. Instead, a few dozen "dollar millionaires," domestic and foreign, have made huge profits. Experts estimate that the unregulated [illegal] import of alcohol alone deprives the state of 18–20 trillion rubles a year.

Finally, one more source is people's savings, which are estimated by experts to amount to some 20 billion dollars in cash, that is, twice as much as the whole three-year IMF credit. This money could be used to boost domestic production if we could only develop secure investment mechanisms guaranteed by the state.

The simplest and probably most effective mechanism is a system of housing saving banks. In Germany, such banks helped rapidly overcome the country's post–World War II destruction, solve the acute housing shortage, and incorporate people's savings into production turnover. Construction, especially housing construction, is a powerful accelerator for the entire economy. The fact that we have not taken advantage of this potential, which has been proved to work in other parts of the world, shows once again the lack of ability or desire on the part of Yeltsin and his government to solve concrete problems.

It is true that people today simple do not trust this government with their savings after the giant voucher scam of 1992,[3] and they are unlikely to entrust their money to it again. By now, everyone knows that the words of Yeltsin and his team cannot be taken seriously, that their promises cannot be believed, and that their guarantees cannot be relied upon. This is one more reason why the ruling elite must be replaced: it has used up its credit of confidence with the people, and people's confidence is the most important element of the economy.

Activating the mechanisms outlined above would be enough for achieving rapid positive results. The fly-wheel of Russia's production will then begin to turn with increasing speed and bring prosperity to our citizens. There are no utopias in this. All of this can be done today!

Election Platform, June 1996

Russia, Motherland, People

Citizens of Russia! Compatriots!

The time for responsible decisions is here. The choice on June 16 will determine Russia's fate for many years to come. In entering the contest for the office of President of the Russian Federation, I feel obligated to tell you what inclined me to take this step.

I was born at the end of the Great Patriotic War in the area of Orel, which had suffered so many wounds. My parents were village teachers. My entire family worked from dawn to dusk and honestly defended our Nation. None of us ever lied to or betrayed anyone. My everyday motto is to know and to act.

I am Russian by blood and spirit, and I love my Native Land. I joined the Communist Party believing that the communist idea, which is more than two thousand years old, most profoundly expresses our people's needs and hopes. This idea resonates with the age-old Russian traditions of communality and collectivism and corresponds with the basic interests of our Fatherland.

The highest purpose of my life is to serve Russia, its people, and the ideals of goodness and justice. I respect the millennium-long history of my ancestors. The fate of all the peoples living on the vast expanses from the Baltic Sea to the Pacific Ocean are close to my heart. I know first-hand how difficult it is for a peasant in Central Russia, a machine builder in the Urals, a miner in the Kuzbass, and a sailor in the Far East to make a living. I have visited every part of our land, met with all kinds of people, tried to give a hand whenever I could. But never before—not even during the aftermath of World War II—have I seen so much grief or heard so many complaints and requests for help as now. My heart aches when I see what is happening around me.

Our Fatherland Is in Danger!

Our people have had to endure a great deal. But we have managed to overcome all troubles and hardships by drawing strength from our native land and our Fatherland, which we hold higher than anything else in the world. What is happening now is the most terrible thing imaginable: an attempt is being made to destroy the source of our vitality and to take away our Fatherland.

Just think:

Our Fatherland is a country, a state, and a nation. Where is our country now? The Soviet Union has been illegally dismembered, suddenly making 25 million of our compatriots into aliens in their own land. The Russian nation has become a divided nation for the first time in its history.

Our Fatherland is family, children, and future generations. But our women have been humiliated and their right to become mothers has been threatened because a majority of families cannot afford to have children. Children have been deprived of virtually everything they had very recently. Man's sacred right to life is no longer protected. Russia is physically dying out at the rate of a million persons per year!

Our Fatherland is the link between generations. It is respect for the elderly and care for their well-being and spiritual joy and peace. Today, the veterans who defended our Native Land and then rebuilt it from scratch to the level of a world power have been tossed to the vagaries of fate.

Our Fatherland is the indivisible property of its citizens. But the majority of our people are being driven into poverty and are being deprived of their right to use the wealth of their country. Everything is being pilfered and taken abroad by insatiable predators. They are now even making a grab for our common property, given to us by nature: our land and its mineral riches.

Our Fatherland is people's ability to associate with each other. But people can no longer afford to travel to visit family or friends for a wedding or even a funeral. Many do not have enough money to make a long-distance phone call, go to the theater, or even buy a book.

Our Fatherland is tradition, culture, and language. But we are witnessing an unprecedented assault against the time-honored spiritual values and moral ideals of our way of life. The heirs of a great nation are being brainwashed into feeling like inferiors and second-class human beings. Our nation is consciously being subjected to insults. Attempts are being made to force Russia into a mold that is alien to it and to adopt a cult of profiteering, violence, dissipation, and egotism.

Our Fatherland is national and state independence and respect in the world. But our country is becoming progressively more dependent on foreign powers and losing its allies. During the past ten years, our woeful leaders have incurred debts that it will take our country two hundred years to repay. Our lands are not protected against the import of nuclear waste, trashy goods, "dirty money," contagious diseases, weapons, and narcotics. Who then is living happily and well in Russia today? The Russian language does not even have a name for them. They comprise a tiny minority and are called *compradors*. Their ideal is a rootless individual whose Homeland is wherever there is a profit to be made. Their aim is to remake the entire nation in their own image and likeness. Their tools are money, provocations, corruption, and lies. They are looking for an easy victory over us. They can easily be identified: they are the people who contemptuously call our Fatherland "this country."

Who Is Pulling Russia Back?

Our current authorities claim that the communists and their allies want to return Russia to the past. We cannot go back to the past for the simple reason that we actually never left it. On the contrary, we are sinking deeper and deeper into the most negative elements of the past.

The real reforms that are vitally needed by our country are yet to begin. Let us judge the "democratic" regime on the basis of its deeds. What could it have done? A great deal! And what good has it done? Nothing. The regime has been most consistent in possessing absolute power along with absolute ignorance about what to do other than to destroy.

Who is in charge of Russia today? Former members of the CPSU elite, "shadow businessmen," corrupt government officials, and heirs to the worst traditions of the nomenklatura system. And those who continue to struggle against such traditions are called "enemies of reform" who do not wish to acknowledge positive changes.

But what are these "positive changes"? Production has declined twofold; in those branches on which the scientific and technical independence of our country depends, it has declined five- to sixfold. Capital investments in the productive sectors have been cut fourfold. One-half of the tractor and combine pool has been destroyed. There are more than 10 million partially or fully unemployed people, 6 million refugees, and almost 1 million homeless persons in our country. It is the same everywhere you look.

But we are told that in exchange inflation and the budget deficit have been reduced. This is indeed an "outstanding" success on the part of our government, if one does not take into account that it was achieved through the use of a method that is unheard of anywhere in the world: by not paying people for their work and by not repaying debts. This innovation should be patented posthaste.

Having accomplished this economic feat, we can go on to other "achievements." We are invited, for example, to look at Moscow's stores laden with all kinds of goods. But they "forget" to tell us that one-and-a-half times less food is being sold in our country today than five years ago. The food consumption of 40 percent of our population is below the medically approved nutritional minimum. For these people, even a glass of milk is a luxury.

What we have here is not an abundance of goods but people's empty pockets. Everything has become more expensive except vodka. Who benefits from this? There used to be a joke that in Russia store shelves were always empty but home refrigerators were always full. Today, it is the other way around. And our domestic producers provide for only 20 percent of consumers' needs.

It is said that we now have democracy and freedom of speech in Russia. But it is "forgotten" that the results of the referendum in favor of retaining the Soviet Union were flouted, that there were several attempts to ban the Communist Party and other national-patriotic organizations, and that tanks were used to shoot at the legally elected Supreme Soviet. All this has compromised the legal system, violated our citizens' rights, crushed the dignity of the court, profaned our church, and demeaned the honor of our soldiers.

The state has two mainstays: the people and the law. The ruling regime has killed the law. And in order to save itself, it is enslaving the people. The few political freedoms that exist in Russia today are not there because of the good will of the regime but rather thanks to the resistance of the opposition against repressions. The regime simply does not have the strength to crush the nation's opposition and is therefore forced to make a virtue out of necessity.

Because we continue to be bombarded by more and more lies, we must be vigilant—continued credulity would be fatal.

Let Us Unite for the Sake of our Fatherland

I see that our people are opening their eyes and uniting. I believe that they will be able to take their destiny into their own hands and, like the epic Vanka-Vstanka,[4] rise up to their full mighty height.

It is our task to help the people accomplish this. During the past several years, my task as a citizen and as a politician has been to rally all the national-patriotic forces into a mighty union able to lead Russia out of its catastrophic situation peacefully, without violence and civil war, and then steer the ship of state toward national democracy, justice, economic improvement, and spiritual revival.

Today, this effort has had some fruit: our national-patriotic coalition has been founded. In addition to the Communist Party and the Agrarian Party, several noncommunist, patriotic movements have joined the coalition. The doors of our bloc are open to new members. We welcome all those who care about Russia to join us.

The people's understanding of our efforts is growing, and we received much popular support in the elections to the State Duma and to local bodies of power. Now our society has at its service an active and responsible opposition that is not sitting idly waiting until it gets full power.

In the Federal Assembly, we are striving to pass laws on raising minimum wages, pensions, and benefits and on liability for their nonpayment; on state support for the family, mothers, children, and young people; and on the fight against organized crime and corruption. We have introduced measures to restore state regulation of and support for enterprises in the defense, energy, transport, and agro-industrial complexes, as well as the regions of the Far North. We are in favor of making major changes in existing legislation on privatization, budget formation, hard-currency regulation, the tax system, joint-stock companies, production cooperatives, and labor collectives.

We have forced our rulers to use words that they have forgotten: "justice," "social protection," "strengthening the state," and "integration." But words and promises are not enough. Laws must not only be written and adopted but also enforced. What we need is not merely patching holes and cosmetic changes designed to win over voters but a radical turn of the whole government policy toward real people with their real everyday cares.

Russia Will Come Out of the Crisis

Russia has everything it needs to come out of the crisis and to be reborn as a great power.

Above all, we have people endowed with innate resourcefulness, industry, and rare patience.

We have modern production facilities capable of competing in the world market.

We have very rich natural resources.

We have the spirit of our ancestors, who stood fast under all the blows of fate.

The main problem is that this potential for building our future is now paralyzed and is being squandered. The situation is such that productive work has become unprofitable and, as a result, our labor force is massively losing its skill qualifications. Our high technologies, modern production lines, and scientific schools have been put on a financial starvation diet and are not being utilized. Our natural resources are being squandered, and the profits from them are being stolen and transferred mostly abroad, strengthening the dollar rather than the ruble. We will therefore all have to act under conditions of a severe shortage of time and resources. I believe we must mobilize all our efforts and direct them toward the following key priorities.

First. We must halt the extinction of Russia. All our citizens must be guaranteed the right to work, rest, housing, free education, free medical care, and a dignified old age. Wages, pensions, stipends, and benefits must be brought in line with the real minimum living standard. The population must be compensated for the savings it has lost as a result of the "reforms." The state must again be made responsible for the social well-being of the nation. Special attention must be paid to housing, roads, and the supply of natural gas to houses.

Second. Families, mothers, and children must be supported in every way possible. The position of women in society must be changed drastically by freeing them from heavy work, by increasing maternity leaves, and by providing the necessary financial support. Today, the work of educators and doctors is the advance line in the struggle to save Russia.

Third. Preference must be secured for our domestic manufacturers, whatever their form of property ownership. We must encourage growth in the production of competitive output through reforms in tax, credit, and customs policies and through large-scale state orders and investments. We must do everything possible to ensure that the production of goods becomes much more profitable than brokerage and speculation. Where necessary, we must adopt emergency measures of direct state regulation and control.

Fourth. The peasantry, which is the mainstay of our state and the keeper of the spiritual and moral wealth of our nation, must be supported. We must ensure equal conditions for all forms of farming, both collective and individual. This should be done on the basis of peasants' labor-based possession, leasing, and life-long or hereditary use, but without the right to sell or buy land freely, with the exception of plots adjoining farmsteads and summer cottages, kitchen gardens, and small orchards. Our modern-day Mikula Selyaninovich can and will feed his entire people.[5]

Fifth. The scientific, technical, and cultural potential of our country must be saved. We must give urgent state support to the high-technology enterprises of the military-industrial complex and other branches. We must preserve our public education system and basic sciences, culture and the arts, museums and libraries, the theater and film, without which Russia has no future. We must establish a state system to encourage talent and prevent the "brain-drain" abroad.

Sixth. The financial system must be strengthened. We must guarantee the stability of the ruble with the entire wealth of Russia—gold, diamonds, oil, gas, and ferrous and nonferrous metals. In order to do this, we must restore state ownership of land, minerals, forests, water resources, and the continental shelf. We must also make foreign trade in natural resources and strategic goods a state monopoly.

Seventh. Property relations must be democratized. The branches of industry, energy, transport, and communications that are vital for the security and steady development of our country must remain the in the hands of the state. We are in favor of a mixed economy. All forms of ownership that benefit our Fatherland must have the right to be protected by the state. The rights of trade unions and collectives to exercise control over and participate in the management of enterprises regardless of their form of ownership must also be protected. I emphasize that we are not talking about liquidating private owners but about turning all citizens into the real co-owners of the all-national wealth.

Peace, Order, Safety

All our efforts will be in vain without lasting civil and interethnic peace in Russia.

For my part, I will do everything possible to stop the war in Chechnya and to prevent any future military conflicts on Russia's territory.

Society is a complex organism, and contradictions in it are inevitable. We will resolve them by peaceful means within the legal framework and based on the recognition that Russia's integrity and the security of its citizens are the highest priorities.

The public is being provoked to fear that the opposition, if it assumes power, will take revenge against its political rivals and against those who disagree with its policies. I want to state once again for the record that we will welcome all those who are willing to work honestly, thus increasing the wealth of our Great State and their own prosperity. There will be no redistributions based on ideology and no persecutions based on political views. We are resolutely against repression and historical vendettas. History should be studied rather than denounced.

Our goal is to utilize all the forces of society to overcome the national catastrophe and protect the rights of the person—a goal that cannot be achieved without a broad social dialogue, freedom of activity for political parties, and freedom of opinion, religion, and information.

In the course of such a dialogue, we are ready to propose a broad compromise to all those willing to place the interests of our Fatherland and peace above everything else. Our people will forgive many past transgressions to those who are willing to understand this and who will work honestly for the revival of a great Russia.

We Are for Russia and Russia Is for Us

We must all realize that the greatest threat to civil peace and to our country's security is lurking in the deepening gap between the rich and the poor, when the minority is growing wealthy not by increasing our national wealth but by robbing the poor majority. The continued growth of this group egotism will inevitably lead to a social explosion with the most destructive consequences.

Just as threatening to our country's security is the rampage of crime, especially organized crime. The struggle of various criminal clans to divide and redivide their spoils is the real cause of conflicts like the one in Chechnya. Before you know it, similar situations could develop in ethnically Russian regions as well. Either organized crime is stamped out or our country will collapse.

We want all the peoples of Russia to understand in whose mercenary interests they are being set against one another. Only then can we begin to deal with nationality problems as such, of which there are quite enough as it is. We firmly stand for the equal rights of all peoples and nationalities, and we will protect their legal rights, interests, and needs. But the right of a people to self-determination can be protected only if the responsibility of each people for the state unity of Russia is recognized.

We are in favor of abrogating the Belovezh Agreements, which have caused such immense harm to the economy and security of the fraternal republics. Five years of this shame have demonstrated that no one can overcome the crisis single-handedly. Historical destiny cannot be deceived. Therefore, we have a political and moral right to rescind these agreements. This does not mean, however, that tomorrow someone will be forcing someone else to be annexed or will encroach on someone else's sovereignty. The right to restore the union belongs exclusively to the peoples themselves. We will adopt all the necessary measures for the voluntary restoration of fraternal ties, above all among Russia, Ukraine, Belarus, and Kazakhstan. In this way, we will lay the foundation for a gradual restoration of the union on a voluntary basis.

Our society must be open, but this does not mean that we will allow interference in our internal affairs. We will pursue an independent foreign policy that serves the interests of the Russian state, and we will not hesitate to abrogate unequal international treaties that infringe on the interests and dignity of our Fatherland.

I will strive to ensure the external security of Russia exclusively by peaceful political means. We are against saber rattling, against any self-proclaimed international gendarmes, and against NATO's expansion to the east. But it is well known that you will not get peace by begging for it on your knees. Our armed forces will therefore receive everything they need for the reliable protection of Russia's borders and its interests in the world.

Our army needs not only organizational and military-technical reform but above all ideological and moral reform. A strong army is an army that has a Fatherland, that is sure of its leaders, and that feels socially protected. Our country will have a military doctrine that not only guarantees Russia's national security but also forbids any use of the armed forces against its own people.

Our entire law-enforcement system and special services are in need of the state's particular attention.

The people should not exist for the sake of the government; the government should exist for the sake of the people. Today's "democracy" means mostly that citizens and parties have the right to say anything they want and the government has the right to pay no attention to what is being said. But democracy is the people's power, which means that all state bodies must be answerable to the people. This is what is lacking everywhere in Russia today. The president and his government are not answerable because they are unchecked and the parliament is not answerable because it has no rights. Such a government cannot be strong.

We must change our Constitution and move toward a political system in which the president is not a tsar or a "father of the nation" but rather the highest-ranking official in the service of society, subject to control by and accountable to the representatives of the people.

Not a single minister should be appointed without the approval of the legislative branch. No national program should be commissioned without being first approved by the parliament and a Supreme Intellectual Council. The parliament and its deputies, in turn, must be subject to the control of and answerable to their electorates. We will ensure regular elections to all bodies of power, from the bottom to the top.

I will adopt all necessary measures to fight corruption in the state apparatus, which will once again be placed under the control of the people. High moral standards will acquire the highest priority in politics. The main goal of our society will be to organize life on the basis of truth, conscience, and justice.

There Cannot Be a Strong Russia Without a Strong State

The extremely important role of the state for Russia has been predetermined by its geopolitical and historical features.

No entity but the state can take care of the defense industry, the energy complex, transportation, communications, the environment, and many others. It is the role of the state to defend the country, protect nature, teach children, treat the sick, help the weak, fight against criminals, and ensure equal rights and opportunities for all citizens. But it is not the role of the state to boss citizens around or breed freeloaders. Our own bitter experience has taught us that total statization sooner or later becomes an impediment to progress.

The essence of my strategy is to give maximum room for the creative energy, initiative, and enterprise of all citizens. The state should not be seen as a "benefactor" dispensing favors to its subjects. The state is there to guarantee that millions of people can work freely and arrange their lives as they please. The state is obligated to make sure that no one prevents people from working freely and from making their own decisions about their destinies.

We will ensure the conditions necessary for all this. These conditions are simple and easy to understand:

• power will be given back to the people;

• it will be profitable to produce goods, to build, to study, and to invent;

• workers will have guaranteed employment, will be paid according to their work, and will participate in management;

• peasants will become masters on their own land and will receive necessary assistance from the state;

• teachers, doctors, engineers, artists, writers, and athletes will again feel needed and important in society;

• women will be able to raise their children with a sense of security about their future;

• children will get back everything that has been taken away from them;

• school and college students will be able to study without charge and to have the vacations they deserve;

• talented people will be able to count on the state's support;

• policemen, procurators, and judges will protect honest people and will in turn themselves be protected by the law;

- military personnel will receive everything they need and will be occupied with their direct business of defending the Fatherland;
- veterans, invalids, and the ill will be socially protected and will be given the attention and care they need;
- the safety of society, the family, and the individual, as well as the freedom of speech and public activity, will be guaranteed;
- refugees will finally find a home and a Homeland;
- victimized depositors will get back their savings;
- thieves will be put in jail.

Our goal is freedom and justice. If these are ensured by the state authorities, free people in a free country will take care of everything else without being told what to do or how to do it.

* * *

I believe that this is what will be. I believe in the wisdom and common sense of our great people. I believe that the people will cast their ballots

For peace and against civil war!
For honest labor and against spongers!
For law and order and against arbitrary rule and violence!
For friendship and fraternity of nations and against hatred and malice!
For truth and purity and against lies and dissipation!
For people's power!
For the honor and dignity of the Great Russian State!

Editor's Notes

1. Gazprom is Russia's quasi-monopolistic oil and gas extraction and export company.
2. Our Home Is Russia is a "centrist," pro-government political party founded by Prime Minister Viktor Chernomyrdin, the former head of Gazprom.
3. Individual vouchers—value certificates—were used during the initial round of privatization in Russia. The measure was very controversial.
4. Vanka-Vstanka (Stand-up Johnny) is a legendary hero of Russian epic poems.
5. Mikula Selyaninovich (Mike the Grower) is a legendary hero of Russian epic poems.

Part 5

A Battle Lost

Reflections on the 1996 Presidential Election

Assembled here are articles, interviews, and speeches published during and immediately following the presidential elections of June–July 1996.

The elections were held in two rounds, on June 17 and July 3. In the June 17 balloting, Boris Yeltsin received approximately 35 percent and Gennady Zyuganov 32 percent of the vote (with about 70 percent of eligible voters participating). Ten other candidates shared the rest of the ballots cast. One of them, former general Alexander Lebed, then entered an alliance with Yeltsin.

In the two-candidate final round on July 3, Yeltsin received close to 54 percent and Zyuganov more than 40 percent of the vote; the remaining 6 percent went to "Neither of the above." Voter turn-out was below 70 percent. Yeltsin was reelected for a second term.

On August 7, 1996, Zyuganov was elected chairman of the new organization of the united opposition, the National Patriotic Union of Russia. He was also reelected to serve concurrently as head of the Communist Party of the Russian Federation (CPRF), the powerhouse of the united opposition.

Zyuganov's Union is an umbrella for more than 200 parties and groups. Allied with Zyuganov are former USSR Council of Ministers chairman Nikolai Ryzhkov (head of the People's Power group), Stanislav Govorukhin (leader of the National Party), Mikhail Lapshin (chairman of the Agrarian Party), Alexei Podberezkin (leader of the Spiritual Heritage group), former Russian vice-president Alexander Rutskoi (head of the Great Power group), and Aman Tuleyev (Regional Communist leader).

—V.M.

On the Eve of the Final Round

Do you have any doubts about winning the elections?

We have no illusions on this score. To stay in power, the present regime is capable of doing anything. Remember how these people, in their drive for power, trampled on the popular will expressed through the [March 1991] referendum and then proceeded to destroy the Soviet Union? And how they resorted to barbarian means to assault the Russian parliament and the Constitution in September–October 1993? The current rulers will cling to power, even if this means violating the legal norms, laws, and Constitution of their own creation.

Is it not true that the communists want to abolish the office of president anyway?

We are, as a matter of principle, against uncontrolled presidential powers. We seek to abolish this institution eventually because it is not in accord with the multinational composition and the federal structure of Russia. An obsession with the presidency has resurrected medieval clan politics and the primitive lust for power.

Our patriotic forces, however, intend to keep presidential powers intact during the transition period and to use these powers for overcoming the consequences of the change of government, for restoring law and the people's authority in the country, and for resolving the most urgent problems. In concert with a State Duma's majority, the new president will form a government of national trust.

Letter to the Central Electorial Commission (June 27, 1996)

It has now become obvious that all means have been applied to ensure the election of Mr. Yeltsin to a second term as president.

Information obtained from local sources confirms that the leaders of republics and the heads of administrations of regions, territories, districts, cities, and rural settlements have been given direct instructions to get the incumbent president reelected at any price. Many heads of executive bodies have been warned that they will not remain in office if Mr. Yeltsin is defeated in their jurisdictions.

There are documents confirming that similar orders and directives have been given through official channels by several ministries, agencies, and command structures of certain military branches.

Banks and financial-industrial groups have been mobilized to give support to the president's election campaign. Almost all of them have been given a "preelection tribute" ["donation"].

While visiting various parts of the country, Yeltsin has released budget funds for individual territories, cities, enterprises, and organizations, using these donations as "populist" gifts. Altogether, the funds for such "offerings" come to tens of trillions of rubles. This is the money that has not been paid to teachers, physicians, military personnel, and pensioners. Naturally, this improper and illegal practice of spending the people's money is giving rise to protests and outrage among the population.

There is no need to argue that this attitude toward the election campaign flies in the face of Article 37 of the Law "On the Election of the President of the Russian Federation," which states that the sitting president is "not entitled to use the advantages of his official position" during his participation in the elections.

The mass media are being used to conduct an extravagant campaign in support of Mr. Yeltsin and at the same time to attack national-patriotic forces and to promote hysteria and psychosis. The print media and radio and television networks, along with their heads Sagalaev, Blagovolin, and Miroshnichenko, must share responsibility for fanning social conflict and civic confrontation.[1]

Plans for hundreds of mass events and television and radio propaganda shows, prepared by Yeltsin's preelection headquarters, have been sent out to various districts and are to take place with the participation of state officials. This is a gross violation of Article 38 of the law on presidential elections, which forbids the conduct of propaganda by "federal bodies of state power, bodies of state power of subjects of the Russian Federation, and bodies of local self-government, as well as their officials in the performance of their work duties."

Thus the legal requirements guaranteeing equal conditions for all presidential candidates have been ignored, a fact that has already been noted by international observers and that has been entered in their official documents.

In this connection, I am forced to turn to the Central Electoral Commission of the Russian Federation and the mass information media with a resolute protest and a warning that such illegal actions in preparing elections and conducting preelection campaigns may call into question the balloting results in favor of Mr. Yeltsin.

I categorically insist that you adopt urgent measures to put a stop to violations of the law and to ensure truly equal conditions for all candidates competing for the office of the head of the Russian state.

Remarks at a Postelection Press Conference (July 5, 1996)

What do you think of the new political situation?

A two-party system is forming in this country. One, the bloc of National Patriotic Forces, is based on a state-oriented ideology, on ideals of justice, and on a commitment to the strengthening of the Russian state and to the strict observance of legality. The second is the "Party of Power." The so-called "Third Force," about which there has been so much talk, has not materialized. Its leaders acted as if they were part of the opposition, but when the time came to act decisively from an opposition point of view, all of them—from Zhirinovsky to Yavlinsky—essentially merged with the "Party of Power." Now they must be held responsible for everything that is happening in our country.

What about your participation in the new government?

There has been no official offer. If we receive such an offer, we will consider what the government's policy is and whether this policy corresponds to the interests of Russia's people and is realistic. Only after such consideration would we be able to answer.

Is it true that you may be offered the position of minister of labor?

I myself labor from morning to night, but I do not really know what this job—minister of labor—entails. To accept a position that does not allow you to correct the situation, help the people, or help the country makes no sense. Certainly you must understand this very well.

Why did you congratulate Yeltsin?

There are facts that no politician can afford to ignore. It is today's reality that millions of citizens, whether the choice was imposed on them or not, did vote for him. I am obligated to respect our citizens' right and choice. I am obligated to respect the rules that exist in every civilized society.

Do you recognize the defeat of your bloc?

There is no reason to believe that the bloc suffered a defeat. I have said many times that there cannot be victors in a devastated country. You will see the people's mood turning bad in the coming weeks and months. It would be unfair to talk about our defeat, because, given the conditions under which we had to act, we have achieved good results. The National Patriotic Forces bloc has been growing stronger. In the 1993 elections, we were supported by 7 million voters, in December 1995 by 15 million, in the first round of the presidential elections by 24 million [June 1996], and in the second round by almost 30 million [July 1996]. And, on top of this, we did well in the most industrialized regions. Does this look like defeat? And this took place under conditions when the "Party of Power" had everything at its disposal: money, the press, every means of influence. Just look at the elections in Dagestan [an autonomous republic in the North Caucasus]. In the first round, we gleaned 60 percent of the vote, but in the second, 20 percent less. I know the honest and diligent people of that republic, and I am confident that in two weeks the voters there could not have changed their views without the pressure of external forces.

What do you think of Yeltsin's American consultants?

I do not want to characterize this situation. But with so much massively concentrated pressure on the voters even a resurrected Generalissimo Stalin could not have lost this election.

Do you expect mass protests to take place?

I am against street actions. But I cannot exclude spontaneous flare-ups, including massive ones in the near future. The authorities have given many promises concerning salaries and wages, pensions, and stipends that they will not be able to fulfill.

Is it true that you may try to create a new Social-Democratic Party?

We were (and are) a responsible opposition. We said from the beginning that we do not agree with this [government's] course, and we proposed our own package of laws and our own program for the revival of the country. We proposed a mechanism for the formation of a government of people's trust. A new party is not what we need at this moment.

Do you see your election defeat as the end of communism?

Do you think the support of 30 million citizens is a defeat? I do not think so. If this support was earned by our Party, the CPRF, then there is reason to be proud of this Party. This means that the next time we will get 50 million votes, and you will witness that.

Did your bloc make mistakes in the election campaign?

Everybody makes mistakes. Together with our comrades, we will analyze the entire campaign, and we will discuss all the problems with our allies. Already today I have confirmations from all participants in the bloc and all members of the election headquarters concerning the need to strengthen the structure of our bloc further. It will be a major political force with its own constitution, its own program, and its own strategy.

There are close to 200 various parties and groups in your bloc. Will they, in time, be absorbed by the CPRF?

How could a 600,000 member organization [the CPRF] absorb 30 million citizens? We will build a broad all-national conference, broader than any one party. As to the strategy of the Party and its faction in the State Duma—we will meet next Monday and discuss this at an expanded session of the Presidium of the CPRF Central Committee. At that time, we will determine our tactics for the next six months. Our activities will rest on two principles: law and justice.

We Respect the Will of the Citizens of Russia (July 6, 1996)

The presidential elections are over.

We respect the will of the citizens of the Russian Federation. Along with all other Russians, we understand that the success of those now holding power was achieved at a very high price, one that is destructive for the country and that was the result of gross violations of election laws and of the unprecedented mobilization of state means for the personal preelection campaign of B.N. Yeltsin.

At the same time, we should remember that the National Patriotic bloc, which received more that 40 percent of the vote in this election, has confirmed its impressive public credentials. In an infinitely short, by historical standards, three-year period, we rose from a persecuted and semilegal organization to an all-Russia political movement that holds a strong position in the State Duma and that participated in the presidential elections as an equal of the "Party of Power."

I am especially grateful to my allies in the National Patriotic bloc, fellow Party members, and hundreds of thousands of selfless activists who defied the unprecedented campaign of scare tactics, pressure, and intimidation to carry the truth to the people, tirelessly explaining our position.

I sincerely thank the voters who cast their ballots for me. I assure you that we will continue to defend firmly the ideals of peace, all-national accord, and the moral and spiritual rebirth of Russia.

We view the postelection situation and the prospects for the development of the National Patriotic coalition with optimism. The election vividly demonstrated that we are gaining strength with every new step.

Our main slogans today are perseverance, consolidation, and organization.

The election results have clearly shown that the National Patriotic forces are today the undisputed spiritual leaders of Russian society. And we are convinced that the future development of events will further reinforce our positions.

We will always be with the Russians and with the other peoples of Russia in all their trials.

Many important issues confront us. The time of local elections is approaching. We need to mount an intensive effort to make sure that the authorities, who are now in a state of postelectoral euphoria, do not leave our people without bread, heating fuel, and their earned pay. Another urgent task is to fight back the flood of crime and lawlessness now engulfing the country.

A Strong Left Party for Russia

This piece appeared in Nezavisimaia gazeta, *August 2, 1996*

In my opinion, Russia is losing historical time. The process of Russia's colonization and transformation into an adjunct third-rate country is gaining momentum. Russia is losing its sovereignty and uniqueness. The decomposition of the government's authority, the weakening of the public consciousness, and the destruction of all established ties continue. There is evidence of a further criminalization of society, contributing to internal instability. But the main thing that can be seen by all is the fact that the Party of Power's election campaign slogans and promises have already been forgotten. There is mass starvation among miners, some of whom are ready to throw themselves into the shafts of their mines. There is a flare-up of the war in Chechnya. But instead of seriously analyzing the situation, the ruling regime continues to fan an antipatriotic and anti-Communist hysteria and dig even deeper the trench that cuts across our entire country from the Baltic to the Pacific.

In my opinion, the ruling regime can no longer make a realistic and honest assessment of current events. Instead, it engages in constant "reshufflings" of personnel and endless negotiations in the Yeltsin–Chernomyrdin–Chubais–Lebed group, who, I believe, are often defending opposing interests. In general, today we have no honest and open public politics, and there has been no effort to review the results of our recent activities intelligently.

We [the opposition], for our part, are trying to comprehend the current situation thoroughly, keeping in mind both hard facts and perceived possibilities. We well understand that the situation requires a profound and delicate analysis. I have met my colleagues from the Party and the bloc, allies, Duma deputies, important scholars, cultural leaders, and eminent political experts. From them, I have received numerous reports, ranging from geopolitical summaries to detailed studies of the preelection campaign and including evaluations of such major components of the campaign as the role of the mass media, regional and local efforts, the activities of headquarters, and individual approaches.

What Is to Be Done

We are a constructive opposition, and we have already put forward all our proposals. We have a socioeconomic program, and it is up to the new government to include (or not to include) some of our key positions in its official plan for action. We are definitely not talking here about accusations. And we are not afraid of any countercharges. Moreover, we are also aware that any accusations and charges can be misinterpreted and misrepresented by those who can benefit from doing so.

This is not our game. What we want is to prevent our country's freefall in a new Makhno-like[2] situation, (although the chief Makhnovite is sitting on the throne). We want to get out of our complex crisis by peaceful means and in a friendly way.

We all want to build a normally functioning society on the basis of a multi-type economy. This way, every type of ownership would have its own political superstructure. Since we have accepted these rules of the game, we should start thinking what kind of system—a two-party, a three-party or some other kind—we should have in Russia. If we look at the Party of Power with its affiliated organizations, we can see that its place in the political spectrum, most probably, should be to the right of center. It represents a rightist policy that sanctions frantic individualism, wild and barbarian capitalism of Dickensian vintage, and criminal norms of behavior. On the left of center we have several parties representing together a very different approach to life. Since I am leading and representing one of these parties and because I am doing everything to strengthen it, I also want to create a broader movement based on the national-cultural values dear to the hearts of all our people. I know that we do not want to have another war, having fought four of them during this century. We want our children to be healthy and educated and our old folks to be well cared-for and socially protected. We want talented persons to be supported by the state so that they can develop their talent in the chosen field of work, study, or entrepreneurship. We want a spiritual revival of our Fatherland which is real and not just a declaration on a piece of paper. We want the freedoms of speech and faith to be taken for granted and not to be bestowed on us by someone from above. Those are the key positions on which we can unite into a movement. This movement is being built from the bottom up, in a natural way. During the last three years, it has established branches in 27 regions. The branches are legally registered in their jurisdictions and have been participating in local elections with good results. They successfully participated in the recent presidential elections.

The Impact of the Elections

I do not consider elections to be a card game. It is not a game of any kind, but a great responsibility. I am proud and happy to have friends, relatives, and a family who have never let me down. I have known hardships as an unemployed, persecuted, and hunted person. Through all of this, I have been supported by my countrymen and provided for by my native land. Very recently, I had visitors from my home region here in Moscow. Incidentally, during the election campaign, a dozen or two journalists paid visits to my native village to collect negative background information. But even after a few drinks, not a single villager there threw a stone at me. I think, this speaks for itself.

I did try to hide some election campaign information from my immediate family. I had received many threats and intimidations. I also tried to spare my mother some of the vicious lies that came from the television screen and publications. But I am all right. As the saying goes: wear and tear makes one stronger. This is especially true during a Time of Troubles.

Who Voted for Me?

The better-to-do, prosperous regions of Russia voted for me. The entire core of Russia that for centuries has withstood wars, invasions, and raids voted for me. The province in Russia is healthier and stronger than the center.

The entire Cossack belt of Russia [the Southern regions] voted for me. Men and women of science everywhere also voted for me. Among them were staffs of the academic institutes in the Far East, Novosibirsk, Krasnoyarsk—even Moscow.

In all regions, people between the ages 25 and 55 voted for our ticket. And those are the most active people, in general. Among them were many of those who have created their own businesses, are engaged in solid entrepreneurship and who, therefore, need a Russia with political stability and predictability.

Who Voted for My Opponent?

I did not know that the residents of the port cities, raw material regions, large-city millionaires, and criminal wheeler dealers would be so much pro-Yeltsin in their political sympathies. After all, those people cannot help but see how many of their neighbors have sunk to the depths of poverty because of "reforms." Our major cities have mostly become criminal centers. They have been overtaken by the mass moral and social decadence and the degradation of ethics.

A Lost Battle or a Lost War?

We are standing on the field at Borodino.[3] We have not lost and our opponents have not won. We have preserved our forces and opportunities and are confidently moving forward.

The Results of the Presidential Elections in Russia: An Analysis

According to the norms accepted in the entire civilized world, the recent presidential elections in Russia cannot be considered democratic, equal, or honest. From the very start, candidates found themselves in unequal situations. The entire state machine worked for the incumbent President who also received huge financial support including donations from very dubious sources. Numerous instances of open attempts to pressure voters and to falsify election results were noted. We have initiated approximately one hundred criminal cases involving flagrant violations of the election laws.

The mass media led by the radio and television, contracted by the Party of Power and big business, ran a campaign of informational suppression. This fact was duly noted by international observers.

All this notwithstanding, forty percent of the active voters cast their ballots for the candidate of the National Patriotic Forces. This came to thirty million persons. Various analysts estimate that the total could have been as high as fifty million under more favorable conditions and with more active and better co-ordinated efforts.

The most important political result of the elections is the fact that, after five years of wavering and struggling in an atmosphere of political discord, our bloc of National Patriotic Forces has proved its unity and strength. The bloc started as an agreement to put forward a single presidential candidate and then grew to become a serious political force uniting members of most diverse walks of life. It consists of approximately 150 various political parties, public movements and organizations, representatives of different nationalities, religious faiths, social and professional groups and creative associations. All are united by their striving to preserve and revive Russia. Our bloc has been brought forth by life itself. Its creation added about eight million voters to Russia's political left.

A two-party political system is developing in Russia. Its two main forces are the current Party of Power and the bloc of National Patriotic Forces. The so-called "Third Force" does not count for much as an independent political subject and has no prospects under current conditions.

The basic ideas and premises of the program of the National Patriotic Forces have been adopted by practically all candidates for the presidency, including the Party of Power. This testifies to their vitality and relevancy for today's Russia. The Party of Power, despite its victory, can no longer discount the National Patriotic Forces as a major political force.

At this time, Russian society is in a difficult political, economic and social situation. A maximum consolidation of all sound elements, regardless of their ideological positions and political sympathies, is urgently needed. And for Russia's revival we need to have a constructive opposition.

In the course of the election campaign, it became clear that the potential of the bloc and of the parties and movements that belong to it was not fully utilized, especially as it applied to promotional efforts among the non-Communist electorate. At the same time, the sharp narrowing of the spectrum of political preferences, and the shift in the direction of a two-party political system, demonstrated that our decision to extend our base beyond the framework of one party was a prudent and timely move. The National Patriotic Forces can successfully oppose any anti-Russian policy of any political forces, but only on the condition of complete organizational unity and full co-ordination. All members of the bloc are considered to be free, equal, and mutually complementary.

This is why immediately after the elections, the Council of the National Patriotic Forces decided to transform the bloc into a public patriotic movement with its own Program and Rules, leadership structure, and regional organizations.

I believe that the ideology of this new-forming organization must be based on national security, preservation of traditional values, and ideals of social justice, truth and goodness. Of course, it is not possible to create a program that would entirely suit everybody. But the suggested basic values have already become a foundation for our unity.

One of the most important tasks of the bloc will be to form a shadow government consisting of highly qualified professionals capable of standing up to the incumbent government, preparing decisions on all pivotal questions, and drafting appropriate legislative bills.

The coming regional elections of top executives will be a serious test of the potential of the National Patriotic Forces. Preparatory work for the elections has already started.

Sharing the People's Pains

This text is from a speech delivered on August 7, 1996

The Price for the "Party of Power's" Success

The election results reflect the complexity and drama of the situation in Russian society and demonstrate the character and basic directions of the forces involved in its development.

Mr. Yeltsin has been elected for a second presidential term. And, as had been drummed into the heads of voters by the pro-regime analysts, in this manner Russia has avoided a terrible fate. Or, to be more precise, now Russia does not have to face a "Red Time of Troubles," "All-out Famine," "Civil War," and various GULAGs.

However, for some reason, there is not much celebration in the camp of the victors. Nor is there peace and quiet in the hearts of those voters who were intimidated by such frightening warnings as "Vote as we tell you, or they will fetch you," and accordingly agreed to keep Mr. Yeltsin in the Kremlin—or, rather, in the presidential hospital in Baravikha.

To sum it up, Russia has been forced to run one more "penalty round." This is what all of us tried but failed to prevent. For Russia, it means losing more historical time, sovereignty, spiritual and cultural values, and material wealth.

Under Yeltsin's banner and in the name of Lebed, Russia is today being torn to pieces by a dozen of the "Grand Viziers" who substitute themselves for the President. They follow the principle "Today is mine and tomorrow be damned." Examples of this are before our eyes. Here are some figures and facts.

First of all, during the election campaign, the external debt grew unprecedentedly fast—by four billion dollars almost overnight.

Second, during the same time, the internal short-term indebtedness increased by more than 16 billion dollars.

Third, the accumulated non-payment of salaries and wages has reached 30–33 trillion rubles. During the campaign period it increased almost two-fold.

Fourth, Russia's reserves of hard currency in April and May alone have been reduced by one half, from 8.7 to 4.3 billion dollars.

Fifth, because of the monetary policy, combined with budgetary allocations to support the Party of Power's election campaign, Russia's national economy has again entered a stage of decline. Its overall performance cannot even match the much advertised increase that followed the 1995 depression.

On top of all this comes the energy catastrophe in the Far East, mass miners' strikes, terrorism in places where people congregate, a new flare-up of war in Chechnya, a collapsing credit system, and a continuing banking crisis with at least one bank going under every two days.

The government is mired in a very difficult predicament and is dragging the entire country with it. The harsh credit-financial policy is killing production as well as destroying the banking system. Thus, the printing press may have to be used again. But the issue of large amounts of new money would lead to another round of inflation. And if this is not followed by a devaluation of the ruble against the dollar, all export businesses would go bankrupt. And without export there would be no money [hard currency] to buy food and most essential goods. As a result, it would be necessary to borrow more from (and become more dependent on) the IMF, which could (in accordance with Article 8 of the Agreement) re-valuate the ruble. This would completely destroy Russia's monetary balance and raise the possibility of a forced transfer into foreign hands of the resource base of our country as forfeited collateral on the pretext that we did not meet our obligations.

Today, I would characterize our society as a melt-down, a kind of magma produced by the catastrophic explosion of the vast spaces historically formed around Russia. We are witnessing the growth of a sharp opinion split concerning property, territory, and spirituality. Instead of a vigorous multi-faceted economy, we see a complete exhaustion of all types of economic endeavor. The public (state) economic sector has been looted and vandalized. Taxes have choked the collective (stock company) property and business. Even the private sector, which continues to live off the ruins of state property, has been depressed.

Social relations have degenerated. The social "roles" of individual citizens have become mixed. Today, the same person can be employed by an idle defense enterprise, work as a home-based craftsman, and act as a small-time traveling trader. This gives a rise to a major confusion of values, orientations, and political leanings for many people.

We should urgently analyze the extremely dangerous process of alienation from society of large segments of the population. We should try to understand the reasons, dynamics, and, most important of all, consequences of this phenomenon. The number of people affected is very large. They are primarily people in trouble who are forming closed groups of drop-outs living by their own special laws.

Such people's anti-social value systems determine their non-standard behavior which can be easily influenced and manipulated by the electronic mass media. We should remember that the Party of Power, as long as it controls the mass media, can easily find support among this alienated population of beggars, street people, and drop-outs. As a socio-political generalization, it can be said that the current regime in our country is becoming like the traditional two-dimensional world of robber barons and their victims, a world of the super-rich and the desperately poor. This is what causes the criminalization of our society and of its power structure. Historically, similar situations have nourished the total degeneration of societies and led to fascism. We must learn how to deal with these problems politically, ideologically, and spiritually.

As a whole, contemporary Russian society has been transformed from a conscription-distribution type of socialism, into a criminal-compradorian type of capitalism (typical at the end of the seventeenth century) ruled by thieves, which is promoting physical and moral genocide. Instead of the promised life-giving light of "civilization," Russia is sinking deeper and deeper into suffocating darkness.

We note that the current political regime is now much more pragmatic than it was two or three years ago. In those days, the country was openly subjected to the breaking and bending needed to fit the schemes of the most radical liberals. But the current balance of forces in our society compels the ruling politicians, wishing to keep their power, to echo the currently fashionable ideas. The ruling regime is no longer the active source generating political changes. The regime, fighting for survival, is still trying to retain its pro-Western coloring, while at the same time adjusting to the new national patriotic tendencies that now dominate people's consciousness. This gives the national patriotic forces an opportunity to pressure the Kremlin by influencing public opinion on key questions of the day. Our chief weapon in the struggle for people's trust will continue to be clear thinking expressed in truthful words.

Lessons of the Election Struggle

We came through the elections with our dignity intact, especially considering the fact that the forces that were mobilized against us consisted not just of the Party of Power, but much more. We had to face the state machine of a huge country which was illegally turned into an instrument of pre-election support of Mr. Yeltsin. More support came from the mighty international forces that are committed to the preservation of a unipolar contemporary world. For the Russian people, the election became a moment of truth allowing them to judge politicians not by their words, but by their deeds.

The first and, in my opinion, positive lesson of the recent elections is the fact that the event showed that only the National Patriotic Forces could build a powerful political coalition. It was a vivid demonstration of the fact that we have creative potential. The Party of Power, on the other hand, keeps afloat only by the energy of destruction and decay, by generating fear, by depending on bribes, corruption, and criminal dealings.

The second lesson is that the election was an opportunity to demonstrate that we reject power methods of struggle and stand for peaceful competition. We must continue to resist any attempts to use force to solve socio-political problems, even though the worsening situation for ever larger segments of the population threatens to lead to terribly destructive spontaneous disorders.

The third lesson of the elections for us is to be more sure of ourselves. We showed healthy self-confidence. At the same time, we overestimated and even idealized the ability of the voters to come to the right conclusions. As a result, we did not dwell enough in our propaganda efforts on the negative aspects of the current situation in Russia. Assuming that they were self-evident, we did not assert and stress enough the advantages of socialist ideas, and sometimes we felt and acted as if we were "poor relations" in the world of modern politics.

The fourth lesson we should remember has to do with our underestimating the political stamina and vitality of the Party of Power, as well as Yeltsin's desperate determination to cling to power at any price. Hence, we did not expect such an intensive brain-washing effort and negative propaganda to be mounted against us by the mass media.

The fifth and perhaps most important lesson tells us that we cannot rely on our past accomplishments alone. We must grow and perfect all aspects of our work. We must look and move forward. We must learn how to use our reserves more efficiently. The party needs to revise and update its founding documents emphasizing our commitment to true people's democracy, an effective economy, the values of the Russian civilization, and the national-cultural traditions of all peoples of Russia.

How We Can Consolidate Our Position?

First, we should keep in mind that in the foreseeable future we will be dealing with tasks of a general democratic nature, such as the preservation of Russia's state independence, civil peace, individual rights, justice, and freedom of information. We must actively resist any anti-constitutional and illegal policy of the government and employers.

Second, our party must affirm in people's consciousness its image of a responsible, solid, wise, statehood-oriented organization. By our daily deeds, we must prove that we are a constructive opposition which, unlike the ruling regime, could after coming to power pull the country out of the crisis and stabilize the situation. We must convince a majority of our people that we can provide an intellectual leadership.

Third, we must reckon with the fact that Russia's society today is bipolar, and conducive to having a two-party system. Our pre-election coalition represents one of these poles—the left, patriotic party. As such, it is time for us to establish a "shadow government."

Fourth, we must tirelessly work with all social layers and groups, without exception, keeping informed about their problems, interests, demands and activities. We also need to master the modern political, social, and informational technologies used in elections.

Fifth, an important task of our party is to perfect our work in the Duma. It is the duty of our faction there to develop and promote legislative bills that protect the interests of our Fatherland, defend the rights of the working people, strengthen the foundation of democracy, and revive our best traditions. We must thoroughly prepare in advance the work proposed to be done by our faction.

Sixth, we must, on a daily basis, engage in counter-propaganda directed against the anti-people policy of the president and the government. Our work in this area must be constant, without missing even a single instance of their destructive activities.

Seventh, our immediate task is to win local power. Without the powerful support of regional executive structures, we cannot win on the federal level. Everywhere we can, we must establish and strengthen outlets of our influence in the economy, social organizations, and spiritual centers.

Eighth, a key task of our party is to resist the state monopoly on information. The radical mass media represent today a political force far removed from the interests of the people and the state. They are in the hands of people who are spreading lies and promoting propaganda of violence, terrorism, and indecency. We should expect an acute struggle for the access to the main avenues of the mass media.

Ninth, we must attract young, energetic, knowledgeable people. Our pre-election formula 1+1 must become part of our everyday routine.[4] I am convinced that every party member, every supporter of our cause, can convince at least one more fellow-Russian that we are right.

Tenth, we need to know better not only our society, but also our party and the conditions in which it carries out its work. The party gives us our main advantage in the struggle for Russia's revival and the defense of people's interests.

Lastly, we must further promote our relations abroad, strengthen ties with leading international organizations and structures, with parties and movements close to us in spirit. Today, our ideas and actions attract attention all over the world.

Let me conclude by saying that today the powers-that-be understand that they did not win. And we, representatives of the National Patriotic Forces, know that we did not lose. Truth is on our side. And we are armed with the great historical experience of our people.

Today, we could be standing on the field of Borodino at the time just after the great battle had come to an end. We did not blink. And, although the forces attacking us still retain their might, we know what we must do and we are confident that the final victory will belong to us—to Russia, to our Motherland, to our people.

Editor's Notes

1. Mikhail Sagalaev, Sergei Blagovolin, and Igor Miroshnichenko head the three main television networks. All three networks openly supported Boris Yeltsin's reelection.

2. Nestor Makhno (1889–1934) was a Ukrainian nationalist-anarchist leader of a mass peasant uprising in Ukraine during the Civil War (1918–1921).

3. The seemingly indecisive battle at Borodino in the summer of 1812 led to the surrender of Moscow to Napoleon, but also greatly contributed to the eventual defeat of his weakened army.

4. Formula 1+1 means that each member of the active opposition is supposed to recruit at least one of his or her friends to join the movement.

Glossary

apparatchik: a member of the CPSU Central Committee staff in Moscow; often used more generally to refer to a party bureaucrat.

Belovezh Agreement: a document signed at a hunting lodge near Minsk, the capital of Belarus (Byelorussia), in December 1991 by the heads of state of Russia (Boris Yeltsin), Ukraine (Leonid Kravchuk), and Belarus (Stanislav Shushkevich), by which the three agreed to leave the Soviet Union and form a Commonwealth of Independent States.

collective farm (*kolkhoz*): an agricultural producers' cooperative.

comprador: (Spanish orig.) a native businessman acting as an agent of foreign interests.

Congress of People's Deputies: a parliamentary lower house created by Mikhail Gorbachev as part of his political reforms.

CPRF: Communist Party of the Russian Federation.

CPSU: Communist Party of the Soviet Union.

Duma (State Duma): the lower house of the two-house parliament established by the new Russian Constitution ratified in December 1993.

glasnost: "openness," a term for freedom of the press, as introduced by Gorbachev.

instructor: a mid-level party committee official.

NEP: the New Economic Policy introduced by Lenin in 1921 which allowed limited capitalism. It was phased out by Stalin by the end of the 1920s.

nomenklatura: executive positions in the USSR that were reserved for political (party-controlled) appointees.

oprichnina: the secret police created by Ivan the Terrible.

Ostankino: the location of the largest television tower and studio in Moscow.

passionarity: a term invented by Gumilyov to refer to critical, stressful periods in a nation's history.

National Patriotic Forces (Union or bloc): Zyuganov's opposition coalition of parties and groups.

perestroika: "restructuring"—the Gorbachev-era term for reforms.

plenum: a scheduled plenary meeting of top party officials.

Politburo: the ruling group of top party leaders in the Soviet Union.

Russian Orthodoxy: Like other Eastern Orthodox faiths, Russian Orthodoxy developed under the influence of Constantinople and does not recognize the authority of the Roman Pope. Most but not all Russian Orthodox congregations recognize the Patriarch of Moscow, Aleksy II.

secretary: an executive party official in the Soviet Union.

soviet: "council"—an elected executive-legislative organ in the Soviet Union.

Supreme Soviet: the national parliamentary upper house in the Soviet Union.

USSR: the Union of Soviet Socialist Republics (1922–91).

war communism: an early period in Soviet history (1918–21) of martial law and harsh economic measures.

Chronology

1985–1996

1985—Mikhail Gorbachev becomes general secretary of the CPSU, succeeding Konstantin Chernenko (March); initiates reforms; Gorbachev–Reagan meeting in Geneva (November).

1986—Twenty-seventh CPSU Congress (February–March); Chernobyl nuclear disaster (April–May); Gorbachev–Reagan meeting in Reykjavik (October); ethnic riots in Kazakhstan (December).

1987—Yeltsin fired as Moscow's party boss; Gorbachev urges more reforms; Gorbachev–Reagan meeting in Washington (December).

1988—Armenian-Azeri clashes in Karabakh (spring); Reagan visits Moscow (May–June); Gorbachev becomes USSR President; Soviet Constitution amended to establish new parliamentary system and implement other reforms (December).

1989—USSR Congress of People's Deputies elected (March); ethnic unrest in Georgia (April); Gorbachev's visit to China (May); ethnic clashes in Uzbekistan (June); Lithuania's bid for independence (October); Gorbachev–Bush meeting in Malta (December).

1990—Russian Federation Congress of People's Deputies elected (March); Yeltsin quits CPSU (July); ethnic unrest in several union republics; economic decline; constitutional amendments; Russian Communist Party launched.

1991—Referendum on the USSR (March 17); Gorbachev's futile efforts to keep the Soviet Union together; Yeltsin elected president of Russia (June); abortive coup against Gorbachev; CPSU dissolved (August); rise of Boris Yeltsin; Belovezh Agreement (December 8); USSR is formally dissolved (December 25).

1992—Yeltsin's reforms begin; Gaidar's "shock therapy"; mass privatization; growing tensions between Yeltsin and the Russian Supreme Soviet.

1993—START II initialed by Yeltsin and Bush (January); Yeltsin dismisses the Supreme Soviet then suppresses an armed revolt at the "White House" (October); referendum on a new constitution establishing a strengthened presidency and a new parliamentary system; Zhirinovsky's right-wing Liberal-Democratic Party takes the lead in elections to the new Duma (December).

1994—Duma adopts amnesty for leaders of the 1993 October revolt; Alexander Rutskoi and Ruslan Khasbulatov freed (January); $1.5 billion loan from IMF (April); Russian army invades Chechnya (December).

1995—Yeltsin's health problems become evident; united left–right opposition led by Gennady Zyuganov; Communists take the lead in elections to the Duma (December).

1996—Duma denounces Belovezh Agreement (March); presidential elections result in Yeltsin victory, with Zyuganov as runner up (June–July); Yeltsin's health problems worsen.

Index

Gennady A. Zyuganov, a former school teacher from Orel Province, came to Moscow in the 1980s to work for the Communist Party of the Soviet Union and to complete doctoral work in philosophy. Since the collapse of the Soviet Union, he has worked to rebuild the Communist Party of the Russian Federation on his conception of a distinctively Russian socialist superpower. He is now also the chairman of the opposition coalition of "National Patriotic Forces."

Vadim Medish, professor emeritus at American University in Washington, D.C., is an international consultant. His book *The Soviet Union* was published in several editions by Prentice-Hall.